Illustrated SNA

Mark Pataky

WILEY COMPUTER PUBLISHING

John Wiley & Sons, Inc.
New York • Chichester • Weinheim • Brisbane • Singapore • Toronto

Publisher: Robert Ipsen
Editor: Marjorie Spencer
Managing Editor: Frank Grazioli
Electronic Products, Associate Editor: Mike Sosa
Text Design & Composition: Benchmark Productions, Inc.

This book is printed on acid-free paper. ∞

This publication is designed to provide accurate and authoritative information in regard to the subject matter covered. It is sold with the understanding that the publisher is not engaged in rendering professional services. If professional advice or other expert assistance is required, the services of a competent professional person should be sought.

Library of Congress Cataloging-in-Publication Data:

.

Includes index.
ISBN 0-471-19372-0   (pbk. : alk. paper)

Printed in the United States of America.
10 9 8 7 6 5 4 3 2 1

This book is dedicated to Patricia, Christopher, and Meghan, who make my life complete, and especially to Patricia whose help and support made this book possible.

I have spent the last several years educating network consultants, engineers, managers, and businesspeople on SNA, along with the various methods available to integrate SNA traffic across a multiprotocol network. These internal corporate networks, or intranets, provide ubiquitous connectivity to the users of computer resources within an enterprise. The goal of this book is to explain how to integrate 20-plus years of SNA applications into your organization's intranet.

The first questions that may come to mind are, "Why should I care about SNA? Isn't this a dead protocol?" Actually, nothing is be farther from the truth. There are estimates that it would take over a million man years and trillions of dollars to convert SNA applications to TCP/IP-based systems. That's a lot of SNA. What we need to do as network planners and engineers is integrate SNA into the corporate intranet, and preserve the investment in SNA. This book explains the technologies needed to accomplish this goal.

We start by exploring the development of SNA to gain an understanding of its benefits and why it was so popular. You will learn the various SNA terms and gain a basic understanding of SNA technology and the various equipment used to build these networks. We also explore the many technologies used to integrate these systems and enable you to build your network-centric computing environment for the next century.

Let's start by defining *network-centric computing*. Network-centric computing differs from the traditional or legacy data network. The legacy network controlled all of the communications resources. All the devices in the network connected directly or indirectly (through the network) to the central mainframe. Since the mainframe contained all the application programs, this was the "natural" way to build the network. As computers got smaller—first, minisystems, and now the more popular microsystems, or personal computers (PCs)—there was no longer a need to process and store all the organization data in the central mainframe. Distributed processing gave birth to client/server applications.

Network-centric computing provides the connectivity to allow any system within the enterprise to access any application server. The central-site mainframe (or, for that matter, any data processing device) does not control any network resources. This difference forces the network designer, builder, and manager to support a variety of different computing platforms and network protocols. Network users today have an increasing need to access information on multiple computers in a variety of locations. This information not only resides on your organization systems, but also on the World Wide Web (WWW). The Internetwork (along with your internal intranetwork) is becoming an information warehouse. The contemporary network must provide the essential connectivity that enables your users to access the services and information in this worldwide information warehouse.

The intranetwork and those who build it are changing the basis of network design philosophies. No longer is one system or protocol defining the capabilities of the network. Most importantly, combining host-based applications with client/server systems along with inter/intranetworking has dramatically and forever changed the deterministic and predictable traffic patterns. The data network more than ever will be emulating the worldwide voice network, providing ubiquitous *connectivity*.

I often use an analogy of equating contemporary data networks to the old telephone network. The phone network is designed to connect two phones anywhere on the planet. Data networks are rapidly moving to the same model. However, *connectivity*, not *information*, is the goal of the data network. This may seem to contradict the previous discussion, but in reality it is quite consistent.

When I pick up the phone in my office, I can dial any hotel in the world. Let's say I want to go to Japan, so I dial a hotel in Tokyo. The phone system, a smorgasbord of companies and different equipment, connects my phone to the hotel in Japan. The network signals the hotel phone by ringing the phone bell—the phone system provides me connectivity. However, since I do not speak Japanese, and the hotel clerk may not speak English, we may not be able to exchange information. So, communication is possible at the physical or connectivity level, but it may not be possible to exchange information.

The network-centric environment is similar. We need to build contemporary networks that connect any two systems together. However, the language these systems speak and their ability to exchange information is up to the owners of these systems. Your network-centric environment must be able to support a heterogamous computing environment with multiple physical interfaces that speak a variety of languages. The challenge of the network designer is to support SNA-to-SNA communications without having to support a separate network.

This book focuses on two items: First, it provides an introduction of SNA technology, and second, it describes the various technologies available to integrate SNA into an organization's network-centric computing environment. The brief tutorial on SNA discusses some of the historical developments of SNA. This is followed by a discussion on legacy SNA technology, including

SNA addressing schemes and a description of Token Ring networks. The section on Token Ring technology was added because it has traditionally been the primary protocol of SNA LAN devices and the foundation of many of the early integration technologies. Note that while Token Ring networks are important to understand, in no way is this book focused on Token Ring, nor is this the *only* LAN technology available for SNA devices.

You need to understand these various technologies and select the best solution to use for transmitting SNA traffic across your network-centric, intranetwork environment. This book provides a solid understanding of SNA, describes the integration technologies' source route bridging, WAN and LAN encapsulation schemes, and APPN. Thisbook also focuses on the various integration technologies with an indepth dicussion of Data Link Switching (DLSw) and the frame relay solutions, normally referred to as RFC 1490.

So, if you have extensive experience in SNA, read on and learn how the various integration technologies work and how they might fit into your network. If you have experience in the IP or Internetwork worlds, read on to obtain a working knowledge of SNA and how to leverage your IP network to transport SNA traffic.

How to Use This Book

With the amount of information we are forced to consume everyday, it would be nice to simply skim over a few sentences in a paragraph to get the key points of the topic. That is what the Illustrated Network books are about. Each page has a graphic and concise text that makes key points quick to learn and review.

Like all books in the Illustrated Network series, this one is very detailed, yet it is written in way that makes it easy to comprehend. Eighty percent of what is commonly written about is filler information. What this book does is extract the 20% of the required information and places this information in an easy to use format. A similar format is used quite often with training material. As we all know, training must be done is a very structured and concise fashion and it must be delivered within a limited window of time. I have taken this quick learning concept further by using a combination of a text book and a training manual—producing the format of this book.

This book is built specifically to be used as both a reference manual and a text book. There is no reason to read it from cover to cover. A topic can simply be turned to and quickly learned without having to read the whole book.

The back of the book contains a CD. The graphics containing all the key points of the lessons are provided on this CD. You can use the graphics to create a customized training slide show, or use them in a class room setting in conjunction with the book. The files are in a Microsoft Powerpoint presentation. The version of PowerPoint used is PowerPoint 97. Simply start your PowerPoint application and open one of the files on the CD corresponding to the information in the book.

Contents

Part One The SNA Network Overview 1

Part Two SNA Terms and Devices 35

Part Three Network Addressable Units (NAUs):
The SNA Address and Frame Formats 47

Part Four SNA Sessions 69

Part Five SNA Links 77

Part Six SNA LAN Technology 93

Part Seven SNA Integration Technologies 117

Part Eight SNA Summary and Conclusions 201

Appendix DLSw Configuration Notes 221

Index 233

Part One

The SNA Network Overview

Table of Contents

Table of Contents

- The SNA Network Overview

- SNA Terms and Devices

- Network Addressable Units (NAUs)
  The SNA Address and Frame Formats

- SNA Sessions

- SNA Links

- SNA LAN Technology

Table of Contents (continued)

- SNA Integration Technologies
  - Bridging
  - Token Ring encapsulation
  - SDLC pass through (encapsulation)
  - Data link switching (DLSw)
  - SNA Frame Relay
  - Advanced peer-to-peer networking (APPN)
  - SNA Gateways

- Summary and Conclusions
  - Technology Summary and Recommendations
  - Appendix: DLSw Configuration Notes

SNA Growth

3

I often deal with networking professionals who get nervous at the thought of supporting SNA networks. I find several major causes for this anxiety: First, there is a general lack of understanding of SNA and the technologies available to integrate its traffic across an organization's data network. Myths about SNA exist as a result of misunderstandings about this technology. I find this mainly due to a lack of expertise among many networking professionals and the media. This is most interesting since just 10 years ago, the vast majority of an enterprise's traffic was transported across an SNA backbone. The world of networking has changed dramatically over the past 10 years! The personal computer revolution, distributed processing, and the spread of LAN technology has forever changed the face of networking. This change has resulted in new computer processing platforms, new networking protocols, and a new industry of equipment and communications professionals to support these networks.

The lack of expertise in this field is a direct result of the popularity of the Internetwork and its backbone protocol Transmission Control Protocol/Internet Protocol (TCP/IP). Over the past five to seven years there has been a tremendous migration to Internetwork equipment and the labor market has followed as many former SNA professionals migrated into this new area or changed fields in this rapidly expanding market. This left the industry with

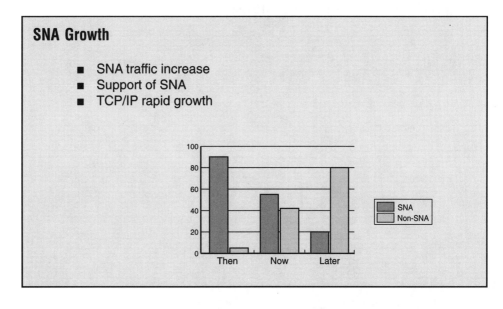

fewer SNA resources and fewer individuals wanting to learn about SNA.

Yet many organizations still rely on SNA as the primary transport for their mission-critical information. In fact, SNA continues to grow in the amount of information it transports, despite many who believed that the mainframe would be dead! Well, the mainframe is quite alive, but its role is rapidly being modified. While still being the predominant SNA processing platform, it is also being positioned as the ultimate IP Web server. Its ability to support vast data processing in terms of CPU cycles, storage capacity, and data integrity, along with a dramatically reduced price, is making it a formidable force in the Internetwork server market.

The belief that SNA application traffic is disappearing because of a whole-scale migration to TCP/IP-based applications is one of the more popular myths about SNA. Although some organizations are migrating away from SNA-based applications, the reality is that SNA traffic is still increasing; however, TCP traffic is increasing at a significantly faster rate! Adding to this is that more and more SNA traffic is being transported over TCP/IP networks, reinforcing the idea that SNA is going away. The result of this network transformation is that a greater percentage of an organization's mission-critical traffic depends on TCP/IP networks. SNA traffic is *not* going away, but is increasing easily lost in these statistics. This presents organizations with the problem of supporting SNA traffic *and* TCP/IP traffic.

The network designer needs to focus on preserving the legacy SNA application. The technology needs to be understood along with the problems it presents. Then the network designer can select the most appropriate technology with which to integrate these legacy systems.

SNA Architecture

4

> ## SNA Architecture
>
> - SNA is a network *architecture*
>   - *Not* a protocol
> - Flexible in adding new technologies
>   - Ethernet and frame relay (for example)
> - Two types of SNA
>   - "Legacy"
>   - Advanced peer-to-peer networking (APPN)

One of the most popular misunderstandings concerning SNA is that it is a protocol. As the name implies (Systems Network Architecture), SNA is actually an architecture. This is a subtle but important difference. As an architecture, SNA defines a series of protocol suites. This provides a means by which to expand basic functionality and enhances the overall capabilities of the SNA network.

Over time, SNA has been modified to support new technologies and new communications protocols. For example, SNA now supports both Ethernet Local Area Network (LAN) and frame relay Wide Area Network (WAN) technologies. The first was rival technology when IBM was touting the benefits of

Token Ring networks. The latter is still gaining in popularity and rapidly becoming the most popular WAN technology.

There are two "types" of SNA. *Legacy SNA*, which supports the traditional mainframe-based networks; and *APPN SNA* ("new" SNA). Legacy SNA is characterized by a hierarchical nodal structure that is based on having the mainframe as the center of the network. All communications resources are controlled by the mainframe and allowed to function only after the mainframe enables them. (In the SNA world, this is referred to as *activating* the resource. We will cover this later.) The mainframe is also the only application host. SNA was clearly designed based on the assumption that communication would exist between a remote device and the mainframe. Products and protocols have been introduced over the years to support computer-to-computer transmissions using legacy SNA protocols, but even these required the central controlling mainframe to enable these communications resources. APPN is a network architecture that supports a client/server model of computing. This model was not popular, or quite possibly not even invented, when the first SNA networks were being installed! APPN is an architecture within SNA that defines a set of protocols to support a client/server networking. It is very similar to TCP/IP, and I often refer to it as a twenty-first century update of TCP/IP. We will discuss the technology and benefits of APPN later.

Routing

5

Another myth about SNA is that it is non-routable. Nothing could be farther from the truth. SNA is routable between subareas. Think of an SNA subarea as a "network." It is similar to an IP subnet. Most networks that introduce routers or bridges to support Wide Area Network communications do not support routing between SNA subarea nodes. An SNA subarea is either a host system or a Front End Processor (FEP).

Most of today's implementations connect either terminal controllers (aka 3174s) or PCs to the mainframe using a FEP. The terminal controllers and PCs do not implement subarea node function and therefore do *not* support subarea routing. The primary purpose of the SNA FEP is to convert the subarea routing frame to the terminal controller (or PC) nonroutable frame. This presents a problem when trying to "route" SNA traffic between the FEP and the remote terminal controllers using multiprotocol routers. SNA "route tables" are built statically in each subarea node. The SNA protocols that "routes" SNA is called *virtual* and *explicit route path control*. These protocols define the SNA route between subarea nodes. The SNA addressing scheme and its implementation on which these are built, are only supported in mainframe and FEPs. Subarea routing is too complex to develop effectively for multiprotocol routers. Since today's routers do not support subarea SNA routing, and the frame that crosses the router or bridged network uses the nonroutable frame format. SNA, is typically referred to as a *nonroutable* protocol.

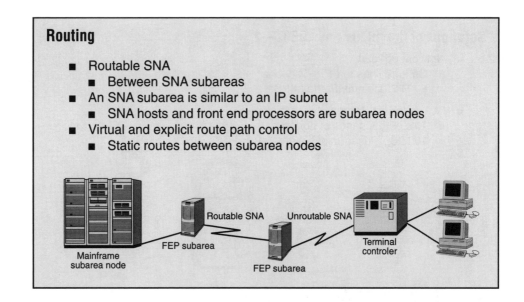

Routing

- Routable SNA
  - Between SNA subareas
- An SNA subarea is similar to an IP subnet
  - SNA hosts and front end processors are subarea nodes
- Virtual and explicit route path control
  - Static routes between subarea nodes

6 Solutions of the 1970s and 1980s—1

The SNA Front End Processor (FEP) was developed to offload processing cycles from the mainframe. (Remember, the SNA architect built SNA as a routable protocol between mainframe and FEPs and between FEPs. The overall intent was to offload the SNA "routing" function from the mainframe.) This made the most sense since mainframe processing cycles were very expensive. Interestingly, though it did offload many of the communications mainframe processor cycles, the data center and mainframe experienced dramatic growth. SNA provided the technology to deliver computer resources to an organization's remote employees. By allowing an organization to build a cost-effective data network, more users gained access to mainframe resources. The result was more and bigger

applications developed for the mainframe. As SNA increased user access, so did the demand for applications, leading to larger and more mainframes.

It is easy to understand why the SNA architects wanted SNA to scale into a very large user network. In fact, the architecture was modified to allow SNA to scale much larger than originally designed. Today's SNA addressing scheme supports 32 bits of network address (or in SNA terms, subareas) and 16 bits of host address (typically terminals in the SNA world). This resulted in massive SNA networks with thousands of communications controllers and tens of thousands of terminals connected into the central data center.

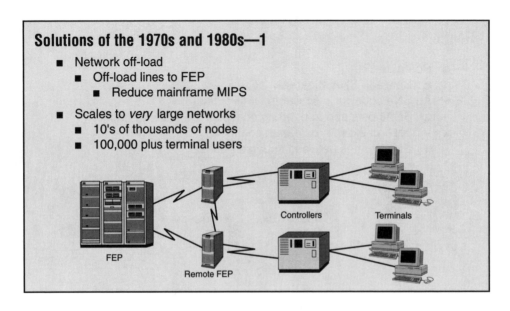

Solutions of the 1970s and 1980s—1

- Network off-load
  - Off-load lines to FEP
    - Reduce mainframe MIPS
- Scales to *very* large networks
  - 10's of thousands of nodes
  - 100,000 plus terminal users

FEP

Remote FEP

Controllers

Terminals

Solutions of the 1970s and 1980s—2

We have dispelled some myths about SNA: It is an architecture and not a protocol; it supports both routable and non-routable frame formats. Now we will explore why SNA was so popular. First we need to understand the telecommunications environment in which it was designed and optimized to perform.

SNA was built to operate in the pre-AT&T divestiture world of telecommunications. This environment is characterized by costly leased lines and analog access facilities. Costly lines resulted in the monopoly granted to AT&T by the U.S. Government. We often view monopolies as bad things that eliminate competition. However, in this case, granting the monopoly

to AT&T provided affordable telephone services to virtually every location in the country. AT&T built the world's most redundant, fault-tolerant, and ubiquitous network in the world. This infrastructure is the United States' Public Switched Telephone Network (PSTN) and is the foundation of all the communications capabilities we have today.

In order for an organization to provide data processing services to its employees, it would typically lease an analog line from the phone company. This line would connect a remote facility to its data center's mainframe. Analog technology, used in phone lines in virtually everyone's home today, are relatively unreliable and slow. A modem (MOdulator/DEModulator)

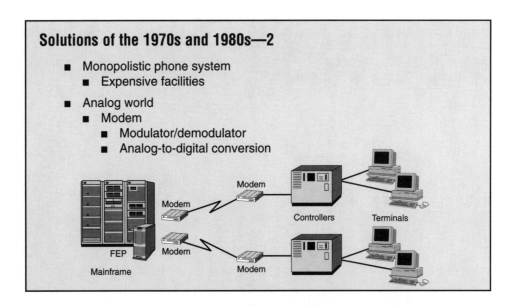

Solutions of the 1970s and 1980s—2

- Monopolistic phone system
  - Expensive facilities
- Analog world
  - Modem
    - Modulator/demodulator
    - Analog-to-digital conversion

is required to convert the digital output from the communications controller, or computer, into an analog signal that can be carried over the public switched network. Early modems were quite expensive, costing thousands of dollars. They were also slow compared to today's performance standards. A medium-speed line would operate at 4800 bps (bits per second), while a high-speed line would operate at speed greater than 9600 bps! Today, most Internet access from PCs is considered slow at 28,000 bps.

Solutions of the 1970s and 1980s—3

In order to provide computer services to these locations, expensive analog lines and communications equipment needed to be installed. IBM optimized this environment by creating technologies and producing equipment such as front-end processors, communications concentrators, computer terminals, and modems. This allowed a business to provide data processing resources to its remote office locations. In fact, any location that could get a telephone could now have a computer access! This was quite a feat in the 1970s.

The world of SNA was built to optimize this environment and provide a "high-performance" computer network. SNA applications used very small transactions. A transaction consisted of a message to the SNA host, typically 10–200 characters of input, and a message from the host back out to the terminal, typically 400–1200 characters.

Since analog facilities were relatively unreliable, several protocols within the SNA suite provided the network with a high degree of reliability and predictability. Error detection and retransmission of missing or corrupted data packets were implemented to insure the network would not drop or lose information. These protocols were implemented on a node-to-node basis, so error detection and correction (the retransmission of lost data) were performed every time data was transmitted between two nodes. This is

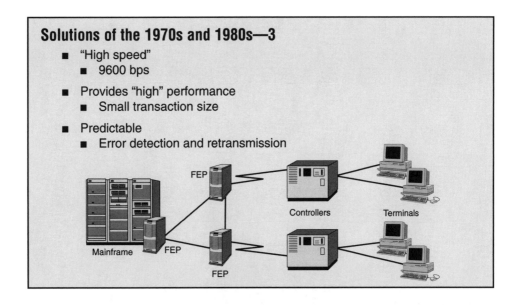

Solutions of the 1970s and 1980s—3
- "High speed"
  - 9600 bps
- Provides "high" performance
  - Small transaction size
- Predictable
  - Error detection and retransmission

FEP Controllers Terminals
Mainframe FEP
FEP

an important concept to understand, since contemporary protocols assume relatively reliable digital transmission paths and assume the end device provides error detection and correction. We will explore this concept later in more detail.

To optimize these expensive communications facilities, SNA used a technology called *multipoint*, or *multidrop*. Multidrop lines are communication circuits that are leased from the phone company and connect multiple remote locations to a central site. Let's look at an example.

Imagine having a data center in New York City, with remote locations in New Haven, Hartford, Providence, and Boston. In order to connect these sites to the mainframe in New York, you would have to run four separate lines from the NYC data center to each of these "remote" cities. This was a very expense proposition.

Multidrop capabilities allowed a single line to be used to connect the data center to these locations. The phone company would run a line from the NYC data center to the nearest location; in this example, New Haven. The circuit would then continue from New Haven to the next nearest location, Hartford. Continuing to build the circuit, it would then connect to Providence, and finally run from Providence to Boston. The result was a single line into the data center at a drastically reduced price for the services. SNA's WAN protocol, Synchronous Data Link Control (SDLC), supported this environment by assigning each location's communication controller a unique "poll address."

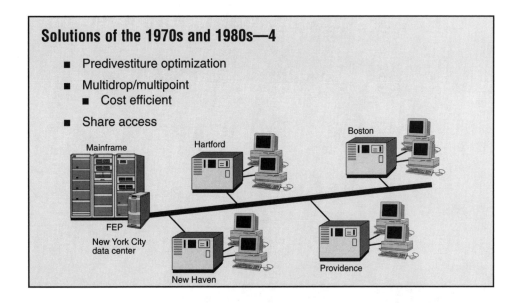

Since all these locations shared this single line, performance requirements limited the number of devices on a single line. The maximum number of locations on a line would be a function of the desired response time and the message sizes and arrival rates from each location. Various modeling tools and services were available to design these networks. While the number of locations on these lines could vary, typically lines were installed connecting four to seven locations.

Another technique used to optimize this environment was remote line concentration. Using the preceding example, imagine the NYC data center having connections to 100 remote offices in California. These offices could have been connected with multidrop lines, but because of the volume of offices and the desired performance characteristics, many lines would still be needed. Also, since these lines had to span the entire United States (from the NYC data center to California), this would be a very expensive network to install. Building a network to support remote line concentration required the use of a remote communications concentrator, a front end processor. In this example, an FEP would be installed at one of the locations in California, which would connect the other California offices using multidrop lines. A single line or group of high-speed lines would then connect this remote California FEP to the NYC data center. Typically, these lines ran at 19.2 or 56 kbps.

Again, this was a very cost-effective way of providing computer access to a corporation's distributed office environment. By installing a remote device in California, an organization would not have to run 14 lines (assuming about 7 locations per line and 100 locations) across the country. Instead these 14 lines would connect (terminate) in the FEP located in California, and the FEP could use a few lines (typically one or two) to connect to the FEP in New York City.

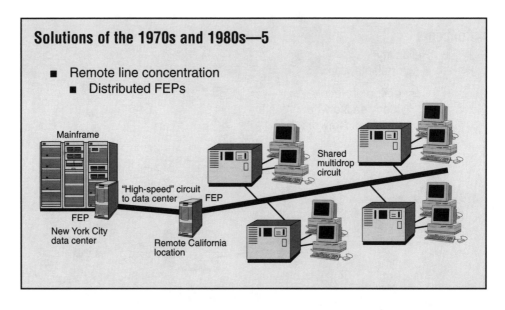

Solutions of the 1970s and 1980s—5

- Remote line concentration
- Distributed FEPs

Mainframe

"High-speed" circuit to data center

FEP
New York City data center

FEP
Remote California location

Shared multidrop circuit

11 Concepts

I stated early that the analog environment was unreliable. Actually, it was unreliable in terms of data transmissions. These analog facilities worked very well for voice traffic, where slight variations in electrical signals might be heard as "static" over a line. However, when transmitting these signals and encoding digital computer information using a modem, these slight variations could wreak havoc with data communications.

SNA used connection-oriented protocols over these facilities to minimize their effect and to detect problems. These protocols provided reliable transmission of data between communications devices. Error detection and retransmission of corrupted data was checked between the terminal controller and the FEP, and between FEPs. This technology was needed in order to reliably transmit information over the analog lines and was very different from the much higher-speed and more reliable digital lines used to connect Local Area Networks together. Today's sophisticated electronics also allow high-speed communications.

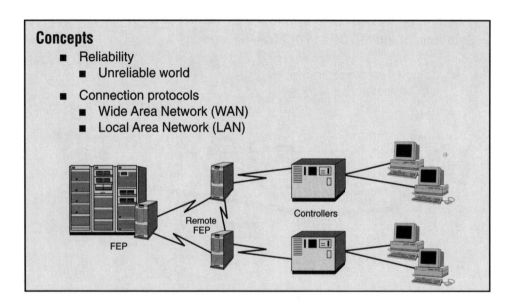

Concepts
- Reliability
    - Unreliable world
- Connection protocols
    - Wide Area Network (WAN)
    - Local Area Network (LAN)

FEP

Remote FEP

Controllers

WAN Concepts

SNA's popular Wide Area Network (WAN) protocols include Synchronous Data Link Control (SDLC) and X.25, with SDLC being more popular in the United States and X.25 more widely used in Europe. Also, frame relay is rapidly emerging as an SNA protocol.

SDLC contains information to assure that data is transmitted reliably between SNA nodes. Features include a cyclic redundancy check (CRC) to detect if any bits are missing or have changed in the SNA packet after being transmitted. It also has a sequence number that assures frames are sent in the proper order and detects any missing frames. When a problem occurs, the receiving device issues a command to have the sending device retransmit any missing or corrupted information.

In addition to SDLC, SNA also supports X.25 networks. These networks are a bit more complicated and sophisticated than SDLC networks, and are not very popular in the United States. X.25 was, and still is, used extensively in Europe. Though having a slightly different frame format, it also has the same error detection and retransmission characteristics of SDLC.

X.25 is a public service offering that guarantees the reliable delivery of data. The X.25 provider delivers an X.25 line (HDLC link

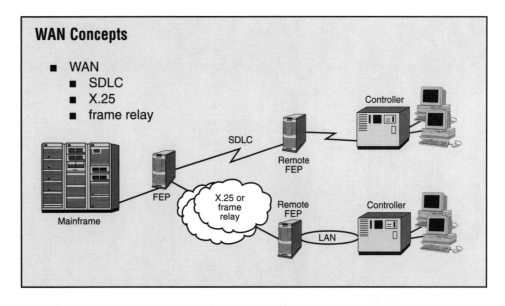

WAN Concepts

- WAN
  - SDLC
  - X.25
  - frame relay

protocol) to the customer premise. The line typically runs at speeds between 4.8 kbps to 64 kbps. The X.25 service provider is responsible for delivering data between subscriber locations. This system is similar in operation to today's more popular frame relay networks.

LAN Concepts

Many people believe that SNA's use of Local Area Networks (LANs) exclusively supports Token Ring; in fact, I often correct individuals who think it is solely an IBM protocol. Ten years ago, this concept was easy to believe as the Token-Ring-versus-Ethernet wars were raging. IBM incorporated Ethernet into most, if not all, of the mainstream SNA products. As an architecture, SNA provided the means for IBM to support Ethernet, frame relay, and several other protocols being used by SNA systems.

In order to support LANs, SNA incorporates similar reliable protocols that exist in the WAN environment. Logical Link Control 2 (LLC2) is a connection-oriented protocol that checks frame sequence numbers to assure that each frame sent is received in the proper order. LLC2 also uses timers to determine if the destination station has received all the packets it was sent. These timers force LLC2 to acknowledge all SNA frames. It is also important to note that LLC2 is used for both Token Ring and Ethernet environments.

A CRC check is made on the entire LAN frame to ensure reliable delivery of information. A CRC check is not provided in the LLC2 header. The LLC2 information is encapsulated in the LAN frame (Ethernet or Token Ring) before it is transmitted across the network. The interface driver performs cyclic redundancy checks and generates a Frame

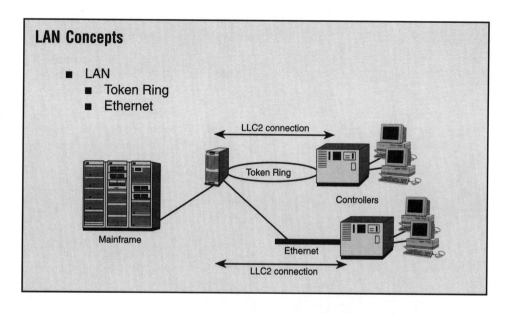

LAN Concepts

- LAN
  - Token Ring
  - Ethernet

LLC2 connection

Token Ring

Controllers

Mainframe

Ethernet

LLC2 connection

Check Sequence (FCS) for the entire frame. The FCS field is checked at the receiving station to ensure that the information in the frame is correct.

Reliability 14

SNA uses LLC2 control for reliable transmission over LAN media. If you have concluded that this is not necessary because LAN media (hubs and internal building wiring) is *very* reliable media, you're right! This presents some problems as we attempt to integrate SNA over a corporate multiprotocol intranetwork. Also, today's more popular TCP/IP protocol along with IPX/SPX and APPN HPR (RTP/ANR) (don't worry, I will discuss these later) perform the same error corrections and data retransmissions. The fundamental difference is that they assume a reliable transmission media and handle error detection and data retransmission at the TCP, SPX, RTP level. Following the Open Systems Interconnection (OSI) seven-layer model, this is layer 4, the Transport layer.

SNA is built for an unreliable world and assumes an unreliable transmission media. It handles error detection and data retransmission at the Datalink layer, or layer 2, of the OSI model.

These differences are important to understand when incorporating legacy SNA in your organization's network-centric environment and provide you with the knowledge to select between the various integration technologies available on the market.

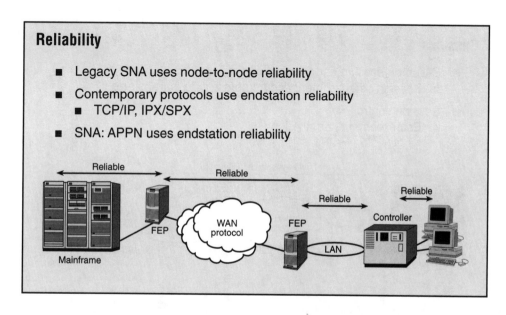

Reliability

- Legacy SNA uses node-to-node reliability
- Contemporary protocols use endstation reliability
  - TCP/IP, IPX/SPX
- SNA: APPN uses endstation reliability

15 Sessions

SNA uses protocols that define the rules by which data is transmitted. These rules use the concepts of a *session* and a *transaction*. A session exists between two SNA devices; in fact, SNA defines multiple types of sessions (discussed in more detail later). These sessions must be established before communications can occur, terminate after the communications are completed, and provide the necessary flow control and reliability mechanisms to ensure the reliable exchange of information. Sessions are also used by SNA to support SNA management of network resources. Typically, an SNA user connects to the "mainframe" by issuing the LOGON command at the start of the business day and terminates the session at the end of the day with the LOGOFF command.

Therefore, a session to a mainframe normally supports a day's worth of business transactions to an application.

A transaction is a message that a user sends to the mainframe, which, in turn, sends a response back to the user. A good example is a bank teller who enters an account number and then receives the account's balance back from the mainframe. SNA has the capability to support multiple transactions and multiple sessions between a terminal and a mainframe.

SNA defines many protocols that allow communication to exist between a terminal (the common device used when SNA was developed) and an application that resides

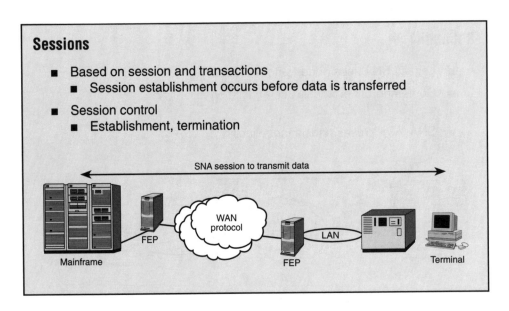

Sessions

- Based on session and transactions
  - Session establishment occurs before data is transferred

- Session control
  - Establishment, termination

SNA session to transmit data

WAN protocol

FEP

Mainframe

FEP

LAN

Terminal

on the corporate mainframe. Some of the more common protocols define the establishment and termination of the SNA session and such items as flow control rules, full or half duplex (which end of the connection can initiate communications), and the size and segmentation rules that apply to the data being transferred.

16 Data Flow

Data Flow

- ■ Flow control
  - ■ Pacing

- ■ Priority
  - ■ Class of Service (CoS)

- ■ Cross-network services
  - ■ MultiSystem Network Facility (MSNF)
  - ■ SNA Network Interconnection (SNI)

An SNA packet uses multiple flow control mechanisms to relieve or eliminate network congestion during peak usage times. SNA *pacing* uses frame window sizes to control the flow of information from the mainframe to a terminal. Pacing is a very complex topic, especially since there are many different types. For example, there is pacing from a mainframe application to a terminal, pacing on the virtual route (routing path), and pacing between SNA nodes. All these flow control mechanisms exist and work independently at the same time.

The session's path is used to characterize data into different priority queues or, in SNA terms, Class of Service (CoS). CoS is a protocol that prioritizes traffic through the network. This provides a mechanism that can mix inter-active terminal data with bulk transmission to printers. Remember that a number of years ago, personal computers were just being invented and definitely *not* being used by businesses. There was no need to provide a priority mechanism for file transfers. This traffic had characteristics similar to print traffic, so when PCs became much more popular in the mid-to-late 1980s, SNA was ready for their traffic volumes. Unfortunately, the slow-speed (4.8 and 9.6 kbps) lines were not.

Finally, MultiSystem Network Facility (MSNF) enables SNA networks to share resources on multiple SNA mainframes, allowing SNA to scale into a large enterprise capable of supporting thousands of users and applications and millions of transactions.

However, MSNF still operates within the confines of a single SNA network. The ability to gateway into other SNA networks is called *SNA Network Interconnection* or SNI. It allows two different SNA networks to communicate directly with one another or use an SNA *internetwork*. This function is similar to today's firewall software, available in routers or standalone processors.

These protocols allowed an SNA network to grow and expand throughout the 1980s. SNA's ability to scale and support vast networking resources is a result of an architecture that can expand in order to absorb new technologies. Today, there are SNA networks that support over 100,000 users.

17 Host-Centric Processing

Host-centric processing is a term used to describe the hierarchical legacy SNA network. It was designed in a networking environment that was characterized by a single data processing platform: the mainframe. End-user devices consisted of nonintelligent devices: the cathode ray tube (CRT), or dumb terminal. A single phone company provided all telecommunications facilities, which resulted in very expensive services. Finally, analog technology was unreliable and slow (because of the electronic capabilities of the time). A single network protocol (SNA), specific management tools, and the ability to monitor traffic patterns lead to performance levels, while not great, were at least predictable.

Another characteristic of the host-centric environment is a data processing environment known as the "glass house." The central site data center built a bureaucracy and moved very slowly to design and implement business applications; often taking as much as 12- to 18-months. Not only was this very unresponsive to the needs of a business, but also very expense to design, develop, and maintain. Very few "canned" business applications existed because of the expense associated with the purchase and support of a mainframe with which to develop business applications.

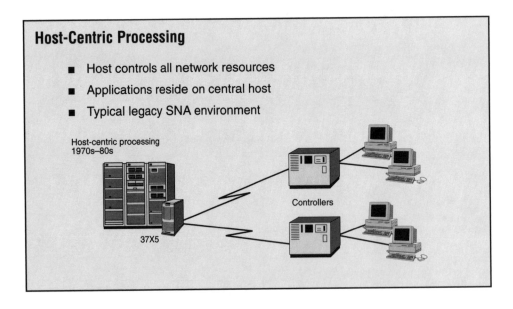

Host-Centric Processing

- Host controls all network resources
- Applications reside on central host
- Typical legacy SNA environment

Host-centric processing
1970s–80s

Controllers

37X5

Distributed Processing

A distributed processing environment followed and was fueled by the technological advancements in minicomputers and PCs. Along with the introduction of lower-cost computing platforms, the networking industry went through a metamorphosis. Local Area Networks (LANs) were gaining in popularity, along with new protocols that allowed PCs to communicate directly with a minicomputer or another PC. The "phone company" and the availability and price of services also changed dramatically. There was competition in the marketplace that not only drove down the cost of services, but provided better access options. Reliable digital lines started to flourish, along with the introduction of new, cost-effective services such as frame relay.

A major driving force to distributed networks was that a corporation's various business units did not have to have the "glass house" data center develop their applications. By purchasing applications for their PCs or minicomputers, businesses were able to respond to business needs in a more timely and cost-effective manner. LANs were deployed to connect various PC clients to a server, and WANs became necessary to network these LANs. The birth of the router industry resulted in the networking of PCs and minicomputers across geographic boundaries.

Corporations started to deploy router-based networks using client/server protocols such as TCP/IP and Novel's IPX/SPX. A new set of

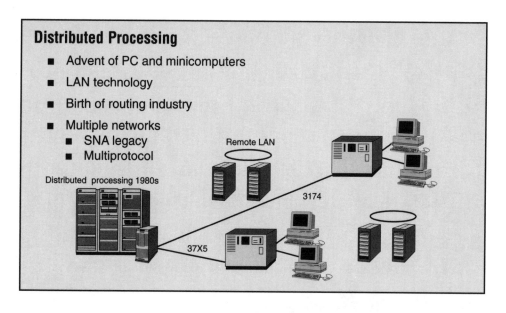

Distributed Processing

- Advent of PC and minicomputers
- LAN technology
- Birth of routing industry
- Multiple networks
  - SNA legacy
  - Multiprotocol

Distributed processing 1980s

Remote LAN

3174

37X5

manager tools and a staff were required to maintain the minicomputers, PCs, LANs, and routers. As the router network began carrying more traffic, companies started to realize a major increase in costs to support multiple data networks built with different protocols that were not easily merged.

Network-Centric Processing 19

The network-centric environment is evolving from the distributed and host-centric worlds. Today, a corporation needs to support multiple application platforms and often several local and wide-area protocols. No longer can one host control the network resources—the network has become the system. An organization cannot afford to maintain multiple data networks in terms of reoccurring monthly telephone charges or the tools and personnel needed to support separate data networks.

The network-centric environment needs to support a variety of protocols. It provides the connectivity between devices. An analogy that I often use is based on the phone company providing this type of connectivity. You can pick up the phone and place a call to a hotel in a foreign country. In a matter of seconds, you will hear the hotel phone ring and, hopefully, answered by the hotel's front desk clerk. In this case, the phone company (or more likely, several telephone companies) processed your request for a connection, determined the locations and routing to that country and city, and finally signaled the phone in the hotel to ring. This is very similar to the way our network-centric data network should work. It should receive the request to establish communications between computers, process that request, and determine how to route the information. However, like the phone example, it cannot guarantee the exchange of information. If the person at the hotel desk and I do not speak the

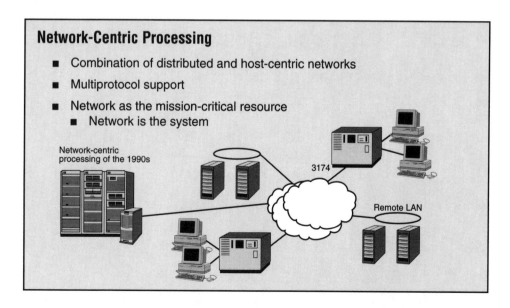

Network-Centric Processing

- Combination of distributed and host-centric networks
- Multiprotocol support
- Network as the mission-critical resource
  - Network is the system

Network-centric processing of the 1990s

3174

Remote LAN

same language, connectivity and delivery was accomplished, but communication was not established. Today's network-centric environment must be able to route information between two computers, but it is an application issue to determine if these two systems can understand the information they are attempting to exchange.

Migrating SNA to the Twenty-First Century

20

> **Migrating SNA to the Twenty-First Century**
>
> - Build network-centric solutions
>   - Multiple protocols on LANS and WANS
> - Preserve IBM investment
>   - Support of existing equipment and interfaces
> - Preserve IBM reliable and predictable performance
>   - Improve performance

A network-centric environment supports multiple LAN and WAN protocols and preserves the investment in existing systems, often called the *leads* and *feeds* (the types of interface and connectors). Most importantly, we need to preserve the investment in application development. If there are many SNA devices and applications in your network, I image that they will remain there for quite some time.

We need to understand the characteristics of the SNA environment and the various protocols that are used and to provide the same predictability of performance. We need to improve on the existing level of response time and maintain or improve the reliability of the network. In the next five Parts, we explore the internals of SNA. You should obtain enough SNA knowledge to understand which integration method is best for your organization. You can then select the optimum technology to use for integrating SNA into your network-centric computing environment.

Part Two

SNA Terms and Devices

Overview of SNA Terms and Devices

21

SNA consists of many TLAs, or Three Letter Acronyms (and many four-letter acronyms!). This can make understanding SNA very difficult, especially when there are multiple acronyms that refer to the same concept, protocol, or piece of equipment. This section uses an "open fire hose" approach to understanding the complexity of terms. Remember that legacy SNA is based on a hierarchy of nodal relationships.

Regardless of the terms, there are three basic node types: Physical Unit type 5, PU5; Physical Unit type 4, PU4; and Physical Unit type 2, PU2. There is a variation on PU2, called PU2.1, which is the basis for APPN. AS/400s are typically PU2.1 devices. While PU2.1 nodes can be and are used in the legacy SNA network, for the proposes of this discussion, they behave in a manner similar to PU2 devices. In addition to the AS/400 minicomputer support of PU2.1 nodes, the AS/400 also supports an older node type defined as a Physical Unit type 1, or PU1. These are older AS/400 terminal controllers and will not be addressed in this book. Additionally, IBM mainframes supported PU1 devices, but there were few devices and it was so long ago (I have not seen one on any system in over 10 years!).

The second concept to remember is that PUs or SNA nodes support SNA Logical Units, or LUs. LUs come in a variety of flavors that will be discussed later in more detail.

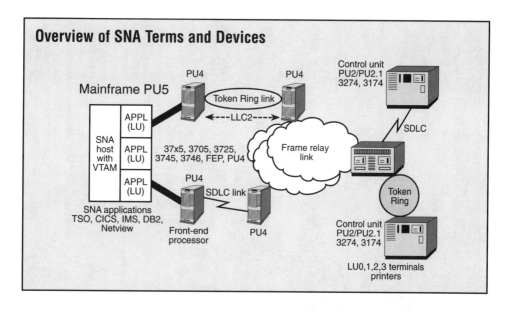

Overview of SNA Terms and Devices

However, it is important to keep in mind that LUs represent end-user terminals and mainframe applications. Virtually all user data are transmitted over LU-to-LU sessions. For the purpose of integrating SNA into your corporate intranetwork, we need only concern ourselves with PU-to-PU communications.

SNA Hierarchy

In the legacy SNA hierarchy, the heart of the SNA network is VTAM, or the PU5. Typically connected to the mainframe through a high-speed channel adapter is the FEP or 3745, the PU4. Routable SNA is used between the mainframe and the FEP, and between FEPs. Connected to the FEP are PU2 terminal controllers. The IBM model numbers for these devices types are 3174 or 3274. PCs or mini-computers often implement emulation software that makes them behave like PU2 terminal controllers to the mainframe. Finally, the 3270 terminal or printer is connected to the controller. These appear as LUs to the mainframe; however, the LU software is actually executing in the terminal controller.

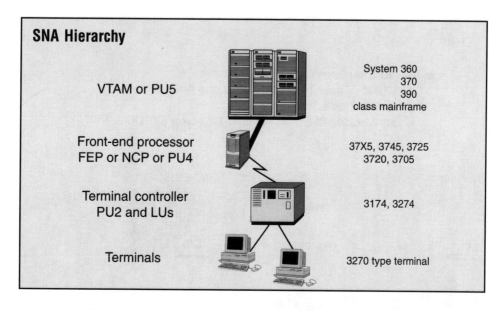

SNA Hierarchy

VTAM or PU5 — System 360 370 390 class mainframe

Front-end processor FEP or NCP or PU4 — 37X5, 3745, 3725 3720, 3705

Terminal controller PU2 and LUs — 3174, 3274

Terminals — 3270 type terminal

23   VTAM

At the center of the legacy SNA network is mainframe software. Remember, legacy SNA is a host-centric processing environment. The mainframe controls all the network resources and is the only application server in this environment. Virtual Telecommunications Access Method (VTAM) is the software at the heart of the SNA network. It executes exclusively on a 360/370/390-class IBM mainframe. In the SNA hierarchy, it is Physical Unit type 5, or PU5, and is the *only* platform that can support PU5 functionality.

VTAM implements routable SNA because it is a subarea node. You can think of a subarea as a TCP/IP network or subnetwork. SNA traffic can be routed between subareas using native SNA addressing. We cover the addressing and frame format of routable SNA in Part Three.

VTAM

- ■ Network center: VTAM
  - ■ VTAM (Virtual Telecommunications Access Method)
    - ■ A subarea node
    - ■ Also called SSCP Physical Unit type 5 (PU5 or PUT5)

VTAM/SSCP/PU5

System 360
370
390
class mainframe

VTAM—SSCP

> **VTAM—SSCP**
>
> - Systems Services Control Point (SSCP)
>   - Controls network resources
>   - Enable/disable (activate/ deactivate)
>   - Controls sessions
>   - Establishment, termination
>   - Processes commands

VTAM is also known as the System Services Control Point, or SSCP. Actually, VTAM software implements SSCP functionality. In the previous part, we discussed resource control and the importance of the SNA session. VTAM's SSCP function is responsible for enabling or disabling the various nodes within the SNA network. In SNA terms, this is referred to as *activating* and *inactivating* the network resources. This is accomplished by either using operator commands entered on the mainframe's systems console or Netview (IBM's host management platform), and it can automatically be accomplished using VTAM definitions.

Sessions are also controlled by VTAM. VTAM processes requests for session initiation by processing commands entered at end-user terminals. These requests are in the form of LOGON or LOGOFF to a particular application. Users typically will enter a simple, one-word request. For example, the end user may enter the application names CICS (a popular transaction processor) or TSO (a time-sharing system). These verbs invoke a command list processor and instruct VTAM to process a LOGON request to a specific application. SNA sessions also need to define the various rules by which two LUs (remember from the previous section that these are typically end-user terminals and applications) can communicate. There is a plethora of possible LU types and rules. The LUs are defined in VTAM definitions, and the various rules are referenced in a number of VTAM tables.

25 FEP

Network Control Program (NCP) is the software that executes in the front end processor (FEP). The terms *FEP* and *NCP* are used interchangeably, referring to the front end processor. The IBM model numbers of FEPs are 3705, 3720, 3725, and 3745 and are used interchangeably to describe the front end processor. (Models 3746-900 and 3746-950 do not run the NCP code. The 3746-950 supports only the new SNA, APPN, and IP routing, while the 3746-900 requires a traditional 3745 running NCP to support legacy devices. These are two newer devices and are exceptions to executing and supporting legacy SNA.)

NCP implements PU4 functionality and requires VTAM, the PU5, to activate and define its resources. The PU4 is also a subarea node, so it supports the routable SNA frame format. An important function of the FEP is that it provides conversion of the routable SNA frame formats to the nonroutable SNA frame formats. This conversion is called *Boundary Function*. Most devices installed in the SNA network today are connected to the FEP (or any other channel-attached gateway, which will be discussed later) and use the non-routable frame format; therefore, SNA is often thought to be a nonroutable protocol. The FEPs can also communicate with other FEPs. Remember that since they are subarea nodes and support the routed SNA frame format, these devices are actually SNA "routers." Unlike many of today's router protocols, SNA

FEP

- ■ Network Control Program (NCP) software
  - ■ Offload telephone lines from the mainframe
- ■ Front-end processor (FEP) hardware
  - ■ Physical Unit type 4 (PU4 or PUT4), 3705, 3725, 3720, 3745, 37X5
- ■ Subarea node (legacy SNA router uses routable SNA frame formats)
- ■ Conversion of routable to nonroutable form of SNA frames

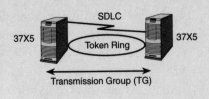

---

paths are based on statically defined route tables. These tables are created by the NCP systems programmer during the definition stage, or SYStem GENeration (SYSGEN) process. These legacy SNA routers cannot reroute traffic around a failed link or FEP. Their forte is reliable delivery of traffic and notification of failed routes to VTAM.

NCP's most popular role is the connection of downstream nodes, the terminal controllers. While it does not establish sessions between itself and the controller or the controller terminals, it does define each controller and terminal within the SYSGEN process. (Remember, in the legacy SNA world, only VTAM establishes sessions or processes requests for sessions between two LUs.)

26 Controllers

The SNA terminal controllers are defined as Physical Unit type 2 (PU2) in the SNA hierarchy. PU2 has been implemented in the IBM products 3274 and 3174. These devices support a variety of interfaces, such as Token Ring, Ethernet, SDLC, X.25, frame relay, and others based on the required connectivity to the front-end processor. They connect the terminals to the SNA network. These terminals are viewed as LUs by the mainframe. It is important to note that the terminal does not have software in it representing the LU; instead, this functionality is provided by the PU software, also known as *microcode*. The most common form of connectivity between the terminal and its controller uses coax cables.

There are many devices that emulate this PU2-type function. Various gateway vendors, including Novell, SAA, Microsoft, Attachmate, and RUMBA have software that makes a PC look like an PU2 to the mainframe. Sometimes these devices are defined as *gateways*, which allow other PCs to connect to them, and they represent a single PU to the mainframe. In this manner, the gateway supports each PC connected to it as an LU to the mainframe. There is an advantage to reducing the number of PUs in the network, since network support of PUs is much more resource intensive than supporting LUs.

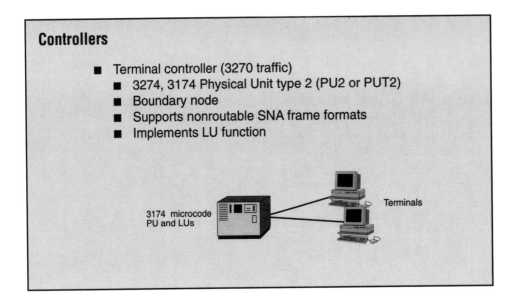

Controllers

- Terminal controller (3270 traffic)
  - 3274, 3174 Physical Unit type 2 (PU2 or PUT2)
  - Boundary node
  - Supports nonroutable SNA frame formats
  - Implements LU function

3174 microcode
PU and LUs

Terminals

Terminals

The simplest device in the legacy SNA network is the terminal. It is often referred to as the *dumb terminal*, simply because it does not have any processing capabilities. Another common term is a *3270 device*. (Note: Sometimes the terminal controller PU2 described earlier is also referred to as a *3270 controller*). The 3270 terminal was an early SNA terminal type. There have been many different types introduced after the original 3270 device, and I could probably fill several pages listing all of them. Instead, we will just use the generic term, *3270*.

The terminals attach directly to the PU2 controller, using a coax cable. The protocol between the terminal and the controller is a proprietary asynchronous connection at speeds of about 1.2 megabits per second. Along with direct terminal attachment, printers are supported directly to the controller with these same coax connections.

The 3270 terminal is the end-user device and is represented as an LU on the PU2 controller to the SNA network. There are several LU types in the SNA environment: LU2s represent terminals, and LU1 and LU3 represent 3270 printers that attach directly to the PU2 controller.

When another device, such as a PC, is emulating a PU2, the emulation software supports both the PU and LU functions for that device.

Terminals

- Terminals
  - 3270, Logical Unit type 0,1,2,3 (LU0,LU2, and so on)
  - 1 to 2 MB asynchronous protocol
  - Coax attached
  - Binds with LU in hosts (LU-LU sessions)

3174 microcode PU and LUs

Terminals

28 Major Nodes

SNA resources are defined in *Major Node Definitions*. These definitions are stored in text format and located in a library kept on the mainframe. The library name is VTAMLST. When a file or major node is enabled (or *activated*, in SNA terms) from VTAMLST, the definitions in this file become available as resources in the SNA network. An SNA node is a PU and should not be confused with the major node.

The resources defined in the major node include Lines, PUs, and LUs. Lines are resources that connect PUs together. The Line resource can be defined as a mainframe channel, Local Area Network such as Token Ring and Ethernet, or Wide Area Network connections such as SDLC, X.25, or frame relay. Since all PUs communicate with one another over a line, this line must be enabled before any other nodes

(PUs and LUs) can become enabled. After the line is enabled, the PU followed by the LU is activated. A successful activation is an indication that the VTAM-to-PU and VTAM-to-LU sessions are established. These are typically referred to as the *SSCP-to-PU* and the *SSCP-to-LU* sessions. As we defined earlier, since VTAM (SSCP) controls all the devices in the SNA network, these sessions must be active before a request from a LU can be sent to VTAM to establish an LU-to-LU session. (Remember that the LU-to-LU session is normally between the terminals and an application. It is this session that transmits user data between terminals and mainframe application programs.)

Examples of major node definitions include NCP, switched node, channel connections, and application definition.

Part Three

Network Addressable Units (NAUs): The SNA Address and Frame Formats

29

Network Addressable Units are SNA resources that exist in the legacy SNA network. These include the lines, PUs, and LUs. The SNA addressing scheme is similar to every other major protocol; it is, however, very complex to implement. This is probably the reason why the major routing venders, including IBM, never provided it as code for their multiprotocol network routers.

We mentioned earlier that legacy SNA is routable. While there are several types of frame formats, or Format Identifiers (FIDs), we will focus on the most common types used in legacy SNA networks. These are the FID2 and FID4. Specifically, a FID defines the frame layout and bit definitions. FID4 is used

between subarea nodes and contains the complete SNA address.

Since FID4 contains the complete SNA address (subarea or network and host), it is routable by nodes that implement the SNA subarea. These include the mainframes (PU5 devices) and the front-end processors (PU4 devices). These subarea devices convert the routable SNA frame format into a nonroutable frame. The FID2 is considered a nonroutable frame because it does not contain information that identifies the network and device to which to send its payload; instead, it contains an address that is locally significant to the controller. The mapping of

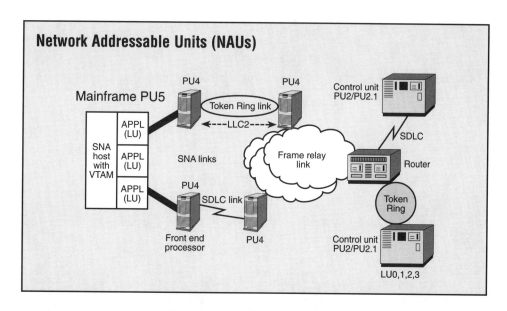

Network Addressable Units (NAUs)

the routable format to the nonroutable format is called *boundary function* processing.

In the following sections, we will explore the legacy SNA addressing scheme and header information. We will understand the difference between the routable SNA frame and the nonroutable SNA frame. This information will help us understand the characteristics of SNA traffic and the difficulties often encountered in integrating SNA traffic into a multiprotocol network. The next 12 slides explore these topics in greater detail.

FID Types

- Format identifiers or FID
- FID0
  - Non-SNA traffic between subareas
- FID1
  - SNA traffic between subareas with no pathing available
- FID3
  - Subarea-to-PU1 frame format
- FID4
  - Subarea-to-subarea routing
- FID5
  - New APPN FID format

The vast majority of legacy SNA node types are PU5 (mainframes), PU4 (FEPs), and PU2 (terminal controllers). The terminal controllers for the AS/400 (a PU2.1) and its predecessor, system 34, 36, or 38, are defined as PU type 1. Subarea nodes, PU5 and PU4, use the FID4 to communicate and support full legacy SNA routing. The PU2 uses a FID2 identifier, while the PU1 uses a FID3. These are several other FID types that we will not describe or go into any more detail on. They have been included here so you can have a reference if you ever come across them.

The FID0 is used to communicate between subarea nodes that support non-SNA traffic. FID1 is used between subareas when the subareas do not support explicit and/or virtual route paths (SNA static routes). FIDF is used to support commands between subareas that support the explicit and virtual routes. Finally, FID5 is a new FID type used to support APPN/HPR communications.

Format Identifier (FID)

- Format Identifier (FID)
  - FID4 subarea routing
    - Subarea and element addressing
  - FID2 boundary transmission
    - Local physical address
  - FID3
    - Old FID type: AS/400's 5294 and 5394
- FEP provides conversion between FID4 and FID2/1

Format Identifier 4, FID4, is the subarea SNA frame type that contains complete SNA addressing information and makes the frame routable by SNA "routers." Remember from our earlier discussion that these SNA routers are the FEPs and mainframes. The frame contains numerous fields that describe the various characteristics of the SNA frame. This information includes session parameters, frame priority, routing information, and flow control. We will discuss the frame format in more detail in the next several sections. The most important fields from a routing perspective are the network and host address. In SNA terms, the network is equivalent to the subarea number, and the host address is equivalent to the element address.

The FID2 is used for boundary node transmissions. This format is used between the PU4 or PU5 and the terminal controller or the PU2. The PU5 or PU4 will convert the FID4 to a FID2. This is true even when a controller is directly attached to a mainframe. Internal VTAM code always produces a FID4. If the connected device is a PU2, which only supports the FID2 format, VTAM will convert the internally created FID4 to a FID2 and transmit it across the channel to the SNA PU2. You can see that this is not a very efficient process. It is important to note that using a PU4 subarea node to support, or *gateway*, the SNA mainframe to downstream terminal controllers requires less mainframe CPU overhead than having the mainframe

(VTAM) directly support these controllers. Later, we will discuss the various gateway options that can be attached to the mainframe channel. One major advantage to the FEP subarea node is that it offloads CPU cycles from the mainframe when supporting legacy SNA.

Finally, the FID3 is used to support PU1 traffic. There are not very many mainframe devices that support PU1; in fact, I cannot remember one! However, this is a popular PU type when attaching a terminal controller to an AS/400. The older AS/400 terminal con-

trollers 5492 and 5493 are PU1 devices. This is important to note, because several of the SNA integration technologies do not support PU1 devices. Interestingly, Advanced-Peer-to-Peer Networking (APPN), which is the native SNA protocol for today's AS/400s, does not support PU1. This presents several problems when trying to integrate PU1 traffic across an intranetwork.

The FEP will provide the conversion of FID4 frame to FID2 (PU2) or, in those very rare cases, to FID3 (PU1). This conversion is called *boundary function processing*.

32 TH, RH, RU

The SNA Format Identifier, or FID, consists of three fields or headers. The first field in the FID is the Transmission Header, or TH. The primary purpose of the TH is to provide the necessary information with which to route an SNA frame to its destination location.

The second field is the Request/Response Header. The header is defined as a Request Header when a message is being sent to request a status or initiate a transaction. The receiving LU of a Request Header normally responds to the request. This response generates a Response Header. The may seem confusing, but the headers are very similar and the request or response is an indication of which way traffic is flowing. Contained in this header are ses-

sion rules, agreed upon when both LUs initiate the session, along with flow control information for this particular session.

The last field is the Request or Response Unit, or RU. Similar to the RH, the Request or Response designation is based on the directional flow of information. The RU contains either user information (real data, which is why we bother with all this other stuff!) or SNA commands and status conditions.

There are many other fields within these headers, and they do provide additional information in order to successfully transmit SNA information. We will explore this in more detail over the next several sections. However,

---

TH, RH, RU

- Components
  - Transmission Header (TH)
    - Addressing information
  - Request/Response Header (RH)
    - Flow control and session information
  - Request/Response Unit (RU)
    - User data or SNA commands

WAN or LAN Header	TH SNA address length based on FID type	RH SNA session information (always 3 bytes)	RU SNA commands or user data (variable length)	WAN or LAN trailer

to get a complete description of these fields and the various SNA LU protocols, I recommend the *SNA Architecture Guide* from IBM. This is a 4-inch-thick book that describes in detail the various SNA headers. It also provides detailed information on SNA session parameters, session flows, and status, to name a few. It truly is the "bible" of SNA protocols.

33

FID4 TH

> **FID4 TH**
>
> - Transmission header FID4
>   - Addressing information
>   - Used between subareas
>   - VTAM: VTAM, VTAM-NCP, NCP-NCP
> - FID4: 26 bytes with subarea/element address
>   - 48 bits destination and origin address
>   - 32 bits for subarea DSAF/OSAF
>   - 16 bits for element DEF/OEF

When you look inside the FID4 Transmission Header (TH) you will see 26 bytes of information. The two largest fields in the header are the destination and origination addresses and consist of a 32-bit network address. The SNA subarea is represented in this field. There is also a 16-bit host address; in SNA terms, this is the *element* address. The SNA element represents all defined resources within VTAM. These include PUs, applications, lines, and LUs. Remember, LUs are typically the end-user terminals and printers, along with representative sessions within SNA applications.

Other important fields include the *virtual* and *explicit* path identifiers. Virtual and explicit routes are the static route definitions that are defined when SNA PU5s (VTAM) and PU4s (NCP) are built by the SNA systems programmer. They are used at session initiation time to allocate a virtual route that flows from the originating subarea (network) to the destination subarea (network). Explicit routes are paths defined between adjacent subareas. So, a session is established on a virtual route, and traffic between the two LUs is transmitted across this path. The virtual route is a static route, and SNA has no reroute capabilities. The virtual route is made up of explicit route definitions. For example, if the originating subarea is 5 and it is sending information to

subarea 15, subarea 10 acts as an intermediate "router." A virtual path is defined between subareas 5 and 15. Let's give this a virtual route number of 1. The corresponding explicit routes are defined in each node and describe how to route information between each subarea, so subarea 5 has an explicit route for virtual route 1 between subarea 5 and subarea 10. Subarea 10 has an explicit route back to 5 and forward to 15, while subarea 15 has an explicit route back to 10. In addition to the route information, there is also a transmission priority that each session can select over a virtual route.

The SNA priority, along with the virtual route, is determined when two LUs request a session. This information is kept in a table

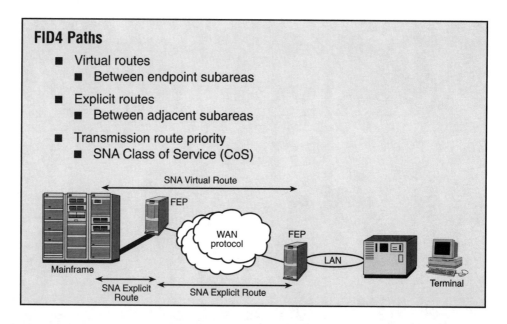

defined when VTAM is started on the mainframe. SNA has four priority queues, three of which are available to user traffic. The highest-priority traffic flows in a network queue that supports PU flow control and network commands. This assures that import flow control (congestion) and commands will receive a higher priority than user traffic to ensure optimal network performance, especially during times of traffic congestion.

FID4

- Subarea (network)
  - Defined at VTAM startup
  - Defined in NCP GEN

- Element (host)
  - Dynamically defined at resource activation
  - VTAM is always element 1

- Symbol Resolution Table (SRT)
  - VTAM maps LU name to subarea/element address

As discussed earlier, SNA is a routable protocol; however, the only devices capable of routing SNA are the FEP and mainframe. Also, the FID4 frame is the only SNA frame that contains the complete and routable SNA address information. The first portion of the address is the subarea, which is defined when a PU4 or PU5 node is configured. The subarea address is configured on the mainframe by the VTAM systems programmer using the VTAM STARTUP parameters. The VTAM startup file is one of the text files we discussed earlier and is located in the library VTAMLST.

The second component of the SNA FID4 address is the element address. The element address is assigned at VTAM startup or NCP system generation. As resources are defined (as in the NCP system generation process) or

enabled through VTAM, an element address is associated with the resource. In either case, addresses are dynamically known to VTAM when the resource is enabled or activated. Address resolution must be coordinated between the NCP and VTAM in order to route and process SNA FID4 datagrams.

Since most SNA resources are known by a name, a table is maintained and coordinated with the FEP to map the SNA resource name to a subarea and element address. The coordination is performed in the SNA host or PU5 using the symbol resolution table SRT. The SRT will map an SNA resource name to the subarea and element address. In this way, SNA isolates the network address from the end users and provides the ability to refer to resources by name.

FID2 TH

- Transmission header FID2
  - Addressing information
  - Used between subarea and boundary node
    - VTAM: terminal controller, NCP terminal controller
  - FID2: 2 bytes local boundary address
    - 8 bits for destination DAF
    - 8 bits for origin OAF
    - 17 bits for PU2.1 devices
      - Local format session ID (LSFSID)

The SNA FID2 is a nonroutable SNA frame. (Note that this is in the context of legacy SNA. APPN changes the meaning of the FID2 address bits and makes this a locally significant label. APPN/ISR uses this "modified" FID2 to route APPN/ISR traffic.) Both PU2 and PU2.1 SNA nodes use this FID type. It differs from the FID4 only in the Transmission Header (TH). Remember that the SNA TH contains the addressing informa-tion. The FID2 TH is only 6 bytes long and has 2 bytes of address. The address consists of 8 bits for the destination and 8 bits for the origin. PU2.1 nodes use a variation of this address. The Local Format Session Identifier (LSFID) bit is used to turn the 8-bit destination and 8-bit origin addresses into a single 17-bit address. The LSFID has only local significance and is used mainly for APPN routing. We will look at APPN in Part Seven.

The PU4, or at times the PU5, will convert the routable FID4 SNA frame format to the FID2. This capability is referred to as the *boundary function*. The destination address has local significance to the controller. It identifies a LU address for the PU. Since the destination and origin address are 8 bits, the maximum number of LUs permitted for each PU2 device is architecturally limited to 256. Since the PU2.1 node uses the LSFID bit, the architectural limit for 2.1 nodes is about 65k.

The local LU address is identified by the LOCADDR parameter in the controller definition. A local address of 02 refers to the first physical port of the controller. Local addresses 00 and 01 are reserved. The local address is defined in either the NCP or VTAM configuration of the PU.

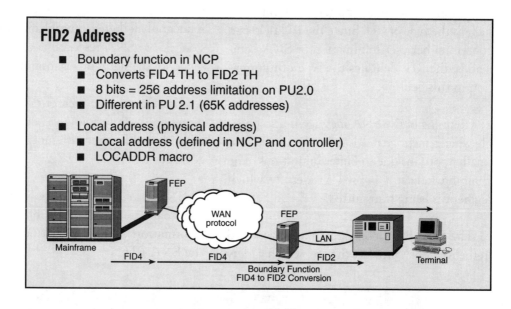

FID2 Address

- Boundary function in NCP
  - Converts FID4 TH to FID2 TH
  - 8 bits = 256 address limitation on PU2.0
  - Different in PU 2.1 (65K addresses)

- Local address (physical address)
  - Local address (defined in NCP and controller)
  - LOCADDR macro

38 Request/Response Header (RH)

> **Request/Response Header (RH)**
>
> - 3 bytes long
>   - Same format for FID2 and FID4
> - Contains session control information
>   - RU category
>   - Chaining
>   - Response mode
>   - Brackets and direction

The SNA Request or Response Header (RH) is the same for both FID2 and FID4 frame types. The 3-byte header contains flow control information and protocol information, such as the type of RU. Since the RU field can contain either user information or SNA commands, the RH identifies the type of information in this field.

Chaining of the SNA message is also possible when a message needs to be segmented into smaller portions due to buffer limitations. The chaining indicator is used to identify which segment is being transmitted.

The SNA Response Mode is also identified in the RH. SNA provides the user with a variety of different types of response notifications: *Definite*, *No*, and *Exception*. Definite requires that the sender is always notified about the status of the transmission. Exception notifies the sender only if there is a problem in the transmission. A No SNA response does not notify the sender of the status of a transmitted message.

The Direction indicator determines which direction the information is flowing. This can be very useful when attempting to debug an SNA session.

SNA provides many tools and protocols that can assure the reliable exchange of information. This information is encoded in the SNA RH.

Request/Response Unit (RU)

> **Request/Resonse Unit (RU)**
>
> - SNA commands/sense codes
>
> - SNA session data
>   - SSCP to LU
>   - LU to LU

The SNA RU is the simplest of fields. The RU will either contain SNA user information or SNA commands and status. The RH described in the previous section identifies the type of data in the RU. This is referred to as the *RU category*. The RU may also contain a Function Management Header (FMH), which contains unique devices or application-dependent information.

40 Frame Formats

There are three basic SNA frame categories: The first is the Basic Information Unit (BIU). The BIU is created by the application and contains the RH and RU information. The application starts assembling the SNA message based on the rules agreed upon at session establishment. This information is included in the SNA BIND that we discussed earlier.

The application passes the BIU to VTAM. VTAM completes the BIU's RH and adds the TH (FID4 addressing information). This creates the second frame type, the Path Information Unit (PIU). The PIU is the completed SNA message that is now ready for transmission to the Channel gateway. If transmission is to a routable SNA node (PU5 or PU4), the message exits the host without being segmented as a PIU. If the PIU is being transmitted to another type of gateway, VTAM must perform an internal conversion from a FID4 to a boundary format FID2. Note that if the frame needs to be segmented, the PIU will contain the entire SNA frame (TH, RH and RU) in the first chain element, while subsequent chain elements will only contain the TH and RU. This example illustrated the FID4 existing as an SNA mainframe. The PIU is also used to describe the FID2 frame existing controllers destined for an SNA host.

The Basic Transmission Unit (BTU) describes the format of the PIU. This is important to ensure the SNA packets arrive in the

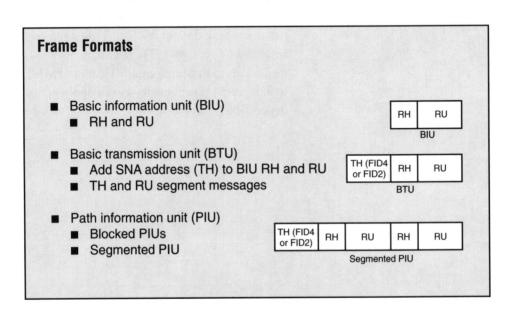

Frame Formats

- Basic information unit (BIU)
  - RH and RU

- Basic transmission unit (BTU)
  - Add SNA address (TH) to BIU RH and RU
  - TH and RU segment messages

- Path information unit (PIU)
  - Blocked PIUs
  - Segmented PIU

same order they were sent. For example, the BTU may "block" several PIUs in a single-channel frame between the PU5 and PU4. The BTU will also define the "segmented" PIU between devices. The first BTU would contain the messages PIU (TH, RH and RU). The remaining BTUs will have single PIUs with the remaining message. These BTUs will contain PIUs with only the TH (SNA address) and RU (the remaining pieces of user data). The RH of segmented PIUs will be eliminated in BTUs. This is required if the message needs to be segmented to support the maximum transmission size of a link.

41

SNI

SNI

- **SNI-to-SNA network interconnection**
  - Requires NCP
  - Cross SNA network
  - De facto "SNA internetwork"
  - Gateways for subarea communication

SNA Network Interconnection (SNI) is a software feature available in the NCP that allows different SNA networks to communicate with each other. SNI can provide address translation so that unique SNA addresses are maintained from network to network. It is very possible (and in most cases, probable) that different SNA networks have the same resource names. This is similar to having unregistered IP networks communicate with one another. SNI can provide the address uniqueness required to preserve the network's integrity.

Performance

```
Performance

■ Performance
  ■ Pacing
    ■ VR, APPL, and VTAM to device
    ■ Based on PIUs, not bytes

■ Class of service
  ■ High
  ■ Normal
  ■ Low
  ■ Network
```

SNA has many parameters that allow the network designer to fine-tune the network. Pacing provides flow control between LUs, SNA nodes, applications, and SNA paths. Multiple pacing parameters are needed and act independently on SNA traffic. Pacing defines a window size in which the sender can transmit a defined amount of BTUs before a response is required. This allows the network designer to determine different flows based on session, LU, and network path characteristics.

SNA also has three priority queues that it uses to send information. The SNA Class of Service (CoS) determines the priority in which traffic will be transmitted across the network. Legacy SNA can only use priority queues between routable SNA nodes. This is because the SNA FID4 contains the SNA priority. When traffic is converted in the boundary function from FID4 to FID2, SNA no longer has the ability to prioritize traffic.

As stated earlier, there are four SNA priority queues: The highest network priority is used to ensure flow control, and network commands can cross the network. The user does not have access to this queue. A user can request service from any of the three remaining queues. Traffic priority is established when the session request is processed. Data will travel in either the high-, normal-, or low-priority queues.

43 Summary

The slide summarizes the various transmission paths across the SNA network. FID4s are used to transport SNA traffic between routable SNA nodes. These include PU5 host nodes and PU4 FEP nodes. The PU4 (and sometimes the PU5) provides a boundary function that converts the routable SNA FID4 format to a nonroutable FID2 format. A FID2 is transmitted between the PU4 to a PU2-type network concentrator. SNA session priority and CoS are supported over SNA-routable nodes.

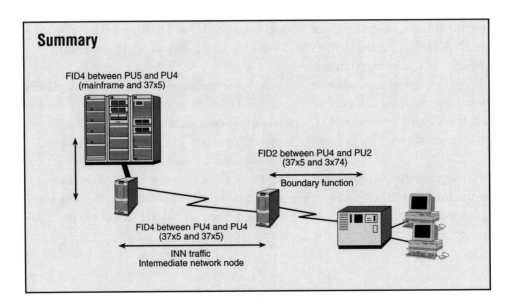

Summary

FID4 between PU5 and PU4
(mainframe and 37x5)

FID2 between PU4 and PU2
(37x5 and 3x74)

Boundary function

FID4 between PU4 and PU4
(37x5 and 37x5)

INN traffic
Intermediate network node

Part Four

SNA Sessions

SNA Sessions Overview

SNA is a protocol based on session establishments and reliable connections. There are three fundamental sessions required to activate a remote SNA workstation or device: the PU-to-SSCP session, the LU-to-SSCP session, and the LU-to-LU session.

SNA Sessions Overview

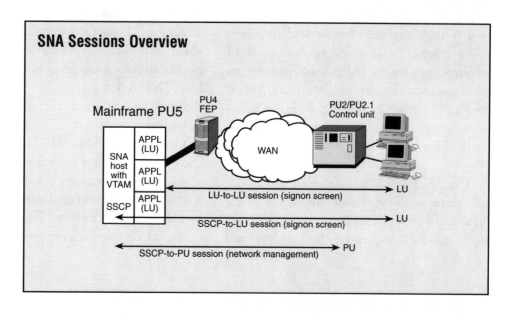

45

Control Sessions

> ## Control Sessions
> - SSCP to PU and SSCP to LU
>   - Between VTAM and the network resource
>   - Network control sessions
>   - ACT/INACT resources
>   - Management

SSCP-to-PU and SSCP-to-LU sessions are two control sessions that are required before a workstation can transmit information to the SNA mainframe. The SSCP-to-PU session is primarily used for network management control. All network management information uses the PU to send and receive management information. Specifically, management commands and responses, or unsolicited events and alarms, are transmitted over the SSCP-to-PU session.

The SSCP-to-LU session provides LU session services. These include the ability to log on to and log off of the SNA host. Control sessions are also responsible for sending and receiving activation or inactivation of resources. Each PU needs to become enabled (or in the SNA world, active) before its corresponding LU can start to communicate. As soon as a PU is activated, its LUs can be activated. When an LU is activated, a formatted system services message is transmitted to the LU. This is known as the VTAM sign-on screen. The user enters a command, which is transmitted on the SSCP-to-LU session and processed by VTAM. VTAM then connects the remote LU to a desired application. The application and remote LU exchange information via a BIND command that allows the LU-to-LU session to initiate. This is the session during which user data can be exchanged.

Logical Unit (LU) Sessions

LU-to-LU sessions, or Logical-Unit-to-Logical-Unit sessions, are used to transmit information between SNA devices. It is required that the Logical Units be of the same type, because SNA information can only flow between like LUs. An SNA application will have a unique LU-to-LU session with each remote device. This can result in applications having thousands of LU sessions with remote terminals. The applications will normally require a definition for every SNA terminal that it can support. These used to be statically defined in various tables; however, most of today's software automatically defines incoming LUs and associates them with a generic profile. For example, a popular mainframe application, CICS, communicating with a thousand terminals would require a separate and unique LU definition for each remote device. A thousand LU-to-LU sessions must be defined and maintained within this CICS application space.

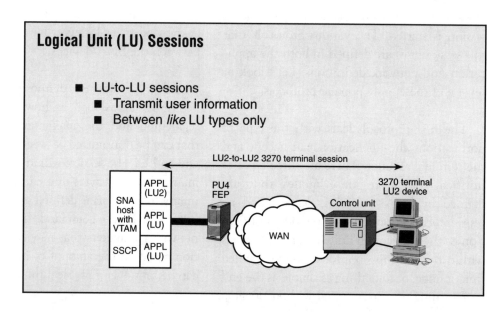

47 The BIND

The BIND

- Sessions initiated with the BIND
- BIND defines the session protocols
  - Profiles
  - Window sizes
  - Duplex
  - Others

LU sessions are initiated with a BIND request. The BIND defines a series of session protocols. The application negotiates these protocols with the requesting LU when a session is started. The various protocols that this session uses are defined in both the application and network definitions. Let's look at several of these more popular protocols.

The first protocol deals with the type of notifications the application can accept and the terminal requires. There are three types of notifications or response modes that are defined by SNA: *exception*, *definite*, and *no response*. Exception response provides notification to the application only if a problem exists within the transmission; for example, a failed link or node, or something as simple as the end user turning off the terminal without logging

off the network. A no response indicates the user session does not require or want any notification concerning the status of the information. Finally, definite response provides an acknowledgment for every message that is sent between the SNA devices.

Other parameters define protocols that determine items such as how information is segmented and the maximum message sizes that can be transmitted between an application and an LU. The session will identify the maximum number of bytes that can be transmitted in any frame. This is defined at session startup using the BIND command. There are other network parameters that may cause segmentation based on the amount of information that can be sent over a physical interface.

Send/Receive protocols also define which LU partner can send. For example, a half-duplex session, which is the most common, allows traffic to be sent one way. The terminal can transmit information to the host and be "locked" until a response is received from the host. In other words, the terminal is not able to transmit information while it is waiting for the host's response.

Part Five

SNA Links

SNA Links Overview

48

In the next few sections, we will discuss some of the most popular links between SNA nodes. SNA defines a link as a physical data path between nodes. These include traditional channel, SDLC, and Token Ring links, as well as some newer links such as frame relay connection.

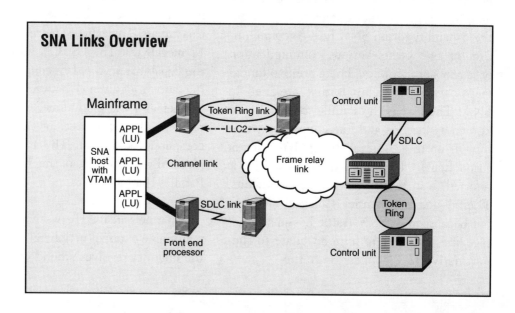

SNA Links Overview

49 Channel Links

The first SNA link that we will discuss is the Channel link. The channel is a physical cable that connects a device to the mainframe. A channel connection provides the capability for an SNA host to communicate to one of its various communication processors or gateways. There are two fundamental types of channels that are used in SNA: The first is the Parallel channel, also known as the Bus and Tag connection, that runs at up to 4.5 megabytes (it has a lot of throughput). Note that channel capacity is referred to in terms of bytes instead of bits. The Bus and Tag channel is a legacy channel, but because most SNA traffic has small message sizes, it is often quite adequate to support native 3270 application traffic.

The more popular channel connection is a serial connection, or ESCON connection. ESCON is a fiber-optic connection using a new fiber-optic cable. The initial versions of this ran at 10 megabytes; newer versions run at 17 megabytes. The ESCON adapter provides the capability in the data center of extending the amount of distance between the peripheral devices and the mainframe, while drastically reducing the "rat's nest" of cables under the computer room floor. The ESCON cable is physically smaller than the Bus and Tag or Parallel channel cables.

Channels are used between a device and the mainframe external peripheral. Our interest in the channel revolves around communications devices. I will refer to these devices by their three basic types: 3172, 3745, and 3174.

A new type of mainframe communication connection has recently become available and is gaining in popularity. It is the OSA-2, or Open Systems Adapter-2. OSA-2 connects the mainframe directly to a LAN interface. Ethernet, Token Ring, and ATM are supported. Protocol support has been limited; initially, only TCP/IP was supported with the ATM connection. APPN has recently been added over ATM in VTAM version 4.4. Legacy SNA is supported over both the Ethernet and Token Ring interfaces. The OSA-2 adapter provides another option for mainframe connection, which eliminates the need for an external gateway. However, today's support should be approached cautiously, since software support, performance levels, and design limitations are not completely understood. Still, this provides an intriguing option for mainframe connectivity and access.

50   Link between FEPs

The front-end processor (FEP), or generically, the 37x5 (3705s, 3725s and 3745s), is a channel attached controller that supports Bus and Tag channel connections. The newer 3745 with a 3746 expansion unit also supports the newer ESCON fiber channel connections. Communications between the mainframe and the FEP use a concept called *Transmission Groups*. Transmission Groups support PU5-to-PU4 connectivity. They are also used with a variety of local and wide-area protocols that connect two PU4s together.

When connecting FEPs together, Transmission Groups are usually made up of multiple lines and have traditionally been SDLC. They provide scaleable bandwidth between remote FEPs and the central data center FEP. SNA transmission groups support multiple lines, even running at different speeds, and the ability to mix media types. For example, this feature gives SNA the ability to connect FEPs together using SDLC and Token Ring links. SNA Link and Interface (Link Station) protocols guarantee proper segmentation and reliable transmission between the FEPs. These links are utilized based on the order in which they are activated. The first link to be activated becomes the primary link, followed by the second link, the third link, and so on. This is important to understand, especially if you attempt to implement a multilink transmission group between SNA FEPs and integrate these connections into your intranet. A scenario can exist in which a lower-speed link is activated before the higher-speed facility. This is more likely if you connect the higher-speed link to your intranet structure and provide a lower-speed link outside the intranet. If both links are activated at the same time, very small latency involved in the high-speed link crossing a router network could result in this link becoming active after the slower but nonintranet link. For example, if a 9.6kbps line and a T1 link connect the two FEPs together, and the 9.6 line becomes active before the T1 line, all traffic will be scheduled initially over the 9.6 link before the T1 connection. The 9.6 link becomes the primary link of the transmission group, so all traffic entering or transmitting between these two nodes would use the 9.6 link over the T1 link. You can see that this would clearly present a performance problem. Care has to be taken when activating the links between front-end processors. In order to ensure that the links are activated in a predetermined order, a "new" parameter is included in the NCP SYSGEN to allow you to identify the order in which links become active. Either use this parameter in the software or monitor the activation of these links.

51

WAN Protocols

WAN Protocols

- Synchronous datalink control (SDLC)
  - Bit-oriented protocol (HDLC)
  - Connection oriented
  - SDLC frame

- Datalink control
  - Logical link control (LLC2)
    - Connection oriented
    - LLC2 frame

Synchronous Data Link Control (SDLC) is the most popular wide-area connection used in the SNA environment. It is a *bit-oriented* protocol based on HDLC, or if you ask SDLC developers, HDLC was based on SDLC. Whatever the case, it is a reliable transmission mechanism that has the capabilities of successfully transporting SNA traffic across the WAN. SDLC is a connection-oriented protocol. A sequence number is assigned to each frame that is sent. A counter is used to keep track of the frames and is synchronized between the sending and transmitting SDLC devices. The SDLC devices compare the number of frames sent and frames received. Since the receiving station acknowledges the frames it receives, a mismatch in the receive counter can be determined by the sending device. This will force sending devices

to retransmit frames that the receiver has not acknowledged. These sequence numbers are used to guarantee transmission between SNA nodes over the link. This provides a reliable transmission medium between nodes on an SNA WAN.

The Send and Receive Count fields are initialized at link activation time using the SDLC command Set Normal Response Mode (SNRM). This command initializes the counts based on modulo 8. However, for PU4-to-PU4 (FEP-to-FEP) connections, SDLC links can use modulo 128. The FEP issues a SNRME (Set Normal Response Mode Extended) command. This is especially useful for high-speed (128–T1) links.

SDLC Multidrop

A major feature of SDLC is its multidrop capabilities. Multidrop is a technology designed to save significant dollars while providing an adequate level of performance for SNA devices. In a world of high-priced communication tariffs, it becomes very cost effective to connect multiple remote sites to the central site data center. The slide shows how a front-end processor in a New York data center communicates with remote sites in Washington, DC, Raleigh, and Atlanta. A single SDLC line connects these four sites together. The line starts in New York, drops to a controller in Washington, DC, goes from Washington and connects to a controller in Raleigh, and then proceeds from Raleigh and connects to a controller in Atlanta. Since a single line is used to connect these three remote locations (instead of three individual lines needed in point-to-point protocols), the cost of communication is significantly reduced.

Multidrop lines only support communication to the master controller; in this case, the FEP. Direct peer-to-peer communications are *not* possible over multidrop lines. In order for the FEP to transmit and receive information from each controller, every device requires a unique poll address. The front end polls each device that allows it to transmit. After a device is polled and information is transmitted, the FEP will poll the next device. A device cannot send data until it is polled by the FEP.

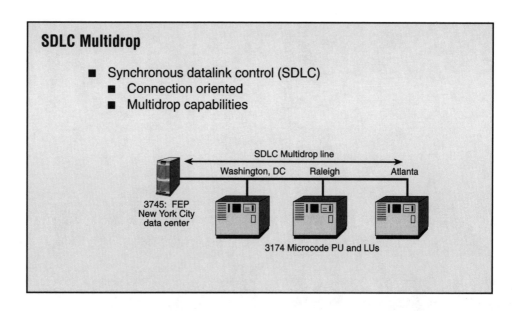

SDLC Multidrop

- ■ Synchronous datalink control (SDLC)
  - ■ Connection oriented
  - ■ Multidrop capabilities

SDLC Multidrop line

Washington, DC   Raleigh   Atlanta

3745: FEP
New York City
data center

3174 Microcode PU and LUs

There are two modes of line operation, *half-* and *full-duplex*. When the line is configured in half-duplex mode, the front end is limited to either sending or receiving information. However, if the facility is running in full-duplex mode, the FEP can poll one device and start receiving data while sending information to a second device. In the previous example, if the FEP polls and starts receiving data from Atlanta, it can also start sending data to Washington, DC. Full duplex allows the FEP to more efficiently control the line.

It is also important to note that the vast majority of controllers cannot send and receive information at the same time. In fact, I have never come across a controller that can work in full-duplex mode; they operate in only half-duplex mode. This does not mean that they cannot be connect to a line operating in full-duplex mode (as in the previous example). Remember, configuring the line or the FEP to operate in full-duplex mode does not imply the remote controller can also receive and send data at the same time.

Other Wide-Area Connections

> **Other Wide-Area Connections**
>
> - X.25
>   - Legacy IBM protocol that is popular in Europe
>   - Defines standards for layer 2 and layer 3
>   - Reliable delivery, but
>   - Typically slower speeds
>   - No multipoint capabilities
> - Frame relay
>   - Rapidly becoming most popular SNA WAN protocol
>   - Similar to X.25, but
>   - Layer 2 only
>   - Cost-effective, higher-speed links
>   - Typically requires FRAD or router

X.25 is a WAN protocol normally not associated with SNA, but it has been supported for over 15 years. X.25 is popular in Europe, primarily deployed as a service by various telcos. It defines standards that include layers 2 and 3 of the OSI model. It is an HDLC bit-oriented protocol, and provides reliable delivery. The standard defines lower-speed links, up to 64kbps, and it is a point-to-point protocol, so it has no multi-drop capabilities, which makes it an unpopular and costly mechanism to use in the United States. Also, because it does some reliable checking and routing of X.25 packets, it has some layer 3 concerns that make it typically slower than some of the other protocols more specifically, SDLC.

Frame relay is a derivation of X.25 and is becoming extremely important in building WANs and migrating traditional SDLC lines to support higher-speed, multiprotocol environments. It is similar to X.25 in that it is a value-added network and is supported by service providers. It is a very cost-effective communications facility and is defined by very high-speed links. Frame relay provides you with the flexibility to support multiprotocol networks when used with a frame relay access device (FRAD) or router that interfaces with the frame relay network.

54   Logical Link Control

> **Logical Link Control**
>
> - Datalink control:
>
> - Logical link control 1 (LLC1)
>   - Token Ring
>   - Ethernet
>   - FDDI
>
> - Logical link control 2 (LLC2)
>   - Connection oriented
>   - Reliable delivery
>   - Based on timers

LAN-connected devices that support SNA use a protocol called Datalink Control. Datalink Control has two protocols that define the type of data being transmitted: Logical Link Control 1 and Logical Link Control 2. Logical Link Control 1 (LLC1) is used with both IPX and IP. It is a connectionless protocol that does not concern itself with the reliable delivery of data. It assumes that a higher-layer protocol will provide these services if they are needed.

Logical Link Control 2 (LLC2) is a LAN protocol that SNA uses to guarantee the delivery of traffic. Although LAN access is very reliable, SNA uses a connection protocol at layer 2 to assure that traffic is delivered reliably and in sequence. Since SNA requires LLC2, it is also used to encapsulate SNA on Ethernet, FDDI, and ATM connections.

LLC2 is similar to SDLC in that it uses send and receive counters. Each station keeps track of the number of frames it sends and receives from each partner. These sequence numbers are initialized at link-station activation using the LLC2 command Set Asynchronous Balanced Mode Extended (SABME). This initializes the field to use modulo 128.

However, regardless of the modulo size, a "window" parameter specifies the maximum number of outstanding frames between two LLC2 stations, or between two SDLC devices. In most LLC2 implementations, I have observed that the window size is typically set to 2, which allows up to two frames to be sent before an acknowledgment is expected. Additional frames will not be sent until an acknowledgment is received by the transmitting device. (Note:

Most SDLC implementations use the maximum window size of 7 frames for modulo 8.)

Connection-oriented networks need to know when adjacent partners are no longer connected to the network. LLC2 supports this capability for SNA-connected devices. It uses keep-alive frames to ensure that its partner is still connected to the network. LLC2 uses timers to implement both error detection and keep-alive frames.

The two timers in LLC2 are Ti and T1. The Ti timer, which is the inactivity timer, is used for keep-alives and is initiated to ensure that the remote partner is active on the network. The Ti timer is initiated every few seconds (configurable to be almost any period of time) since the last time data was received from this partner station. It issues an LLC2 "poll" frame to the partner station. The partner station responds with an LLC2 "poll," verifying that it is still present and a session is still active.

The T1 timer is used to ensure that the packet was received by the destination station. When a packet is sent from a workstation, a T1 timer is initiated on the sending device. This is typically a fixed value and hard-coded in software to be one and one-half seconds. Within that time, the sending system expects to get an LLC2 acknowledgment that the frame was received by the remote workstation.

We will discuss LLC2 in much more detail in Part Six.

55 Token Ring

Token Ring is the most popular SNA LAN and is usually thought to be synonymous with SNA. Token Ring is based on a token-passing scheme that provides each attached workstation with a slice of the bandwidth. A token is generated by a device called a *ring monitor* and is passed to each workstation along the ring. It is the responsibility of each workstation to pass the token to its neighbor. If a workstation has something to send, it will hold the token and put its information in a single frame on the Token Ring. Each device connected to the ring will receive the packet, examine the contents, and transmit it to the next upstream device. This continues until the packet is sent to each device on the ring and ends when it finally reaches the sending station. It is then the responsibility of the sending workstation to remove the packet from the network. When the sending station finishes transmitting its information, it sends the token to the next station. This scheme guarantees that all devices connected to the network have an opportunity to transmit information. SNA is not limited to Token Ring today. This was true years ago, but today SNA runs quite well and is actually becoming more and more popular over other local area connections.

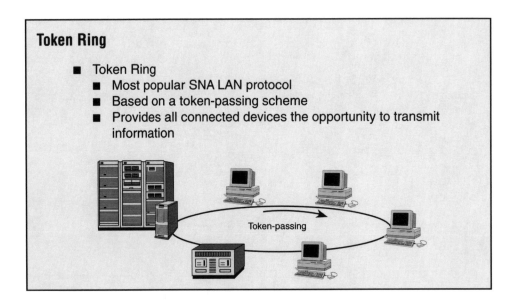

Token Ring

- Token Ring
  - Most popular SNA LAN protocol
  - Based on a token-passing scheme
  - Provides all connected devices the opportunity to transmit information

Token-passing

Other LAN Connections

56

Ethernet, FDDI, and ATM are other LANs that support SNA. Ethernet is becoming a very popular protocol with which to support SNA and 3270 applications. It is especially popular in remote offices. As remote offices start including LAN technology, the cost effectiveness of Ethernet is very attractive. FDDI has become supported for several years, but has received limited acceptance in the marketplace. However, if FDDI is required in your enterprise, SNA will work just fine.

I have included a brief discussion on ATM in Part Six. It can be argued that ATM is both a wide-area and local-area protocol. It is based on switching technology and is a very strategic direction in the SNA world. If you remember in the previous SNA links or channel connections, we saw that an ATM adapter, called the Open Systems Adapter 2, is being provided as a direct ATM connectivity activity to the SNA host. This makes ATM a very viable solution with which to support SNA traffic.

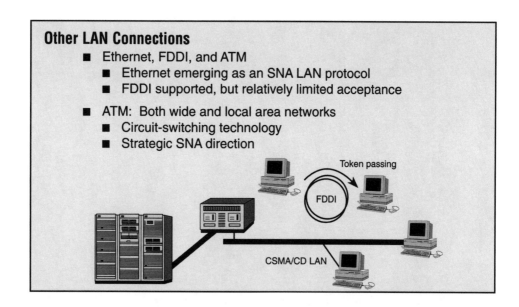

Other LAN Connections
- Ethernet, FDDI, and ATM
  - Ethernet emerging as an SNA LAN protocol
  - FDDI supported, but relatively limited acceptance
- ATM: Both wide and local area networks
  - Circuit-switching technology
  - Strategic SNA direction

Token passing

FDDI

CSMA/CD LAN

Part Six

SNA LAN Technology

SNA LAN Technology Overview

57

In this Part, we are going to discuss SNA LAN technology and devices. I felt that this information should be included in order to understand the LAN requirements of SNA devices and to further explore LLC2. This is fundamental to understanding many of the integration technologies, since most of them are based on LLC2 or have to solve some of the problems with LLC2.

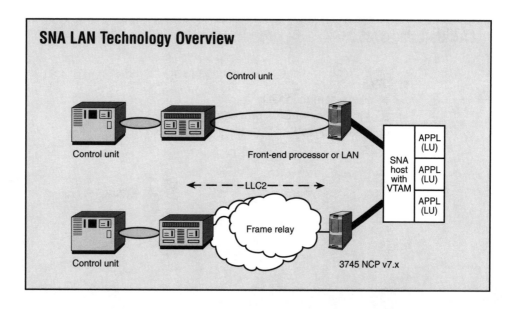

SNA LAN Technology Overview

Control unit

Control unit

Front-end processor or LAN

← – – –LLC2– – – →

Frame relay

3745 NCP v7.x

SNA host with VTAM

| APPL (LU) |
| APPL (LU) |
| APPL (LU) |

58 LAN Gateway 3745

SNA uses several gateways that connect network-attached devices to an application host (the mainframe). The first that I am going to discuss is the Front End Processor (FEP), known generically as 37x5. This gateway provides a connection between LANs and WANs to the SNA mainframe using one of the channel connections. The most prevalent connections are a parallel Bus and Tag, or a fiber-optic serial connection, ESCON. The FEP is clearly the highest functionality of all the SNA gateways. As we saw earlier, SNA is a routable protocol, and the 37x5 is the SNA router. It is the *only* SNA subarea router!

Today's version of 37x5 is called 3745. It is a device that can convert FID4s to FID2s and process all the various frame formats within the IBM world. Software and hardware maturity also makes it the most reliable device available to SNA connectivity within the enterprise. It is the most efficient SNA gateway available, making it the best way to transmit native SNA traffic from either a WAN or LAN interface to the mainframe. The WAN and LAN interfaces supported by the front end are X.25 links, frame relay links, and the most popular SDLC link. Older versions of front ends do not support frame relay, and the oldest front end, 3705, had limited X.25 support. Token Ring is the most popular LAN interface supported on 3745, with limited support on 3725, and no support on 3705. Ethernet and

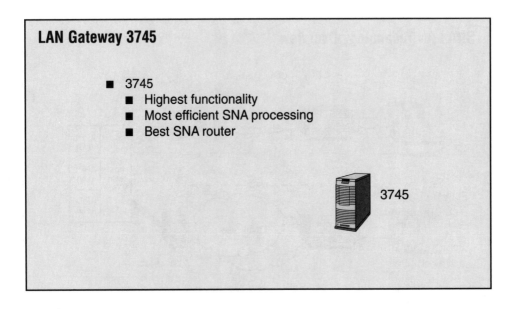

LAN Gateway 3745

- 3745
  - Highest functionality
  - Most efficient SNA processing
  - Best SNA router

3745

ATM connections are supported on the 3745 and 3746-900 expansion frames, respectively.

There are also some issues concerning FEPs, the major one being cost. The FEP can be very expensive to buy and maintain, both from a software and hardware perspective. It was also designed to support only SNA devices. SNA is supported extremely well, but is does not handle other protocols, such as TCP/IP, with the same robustness.

59

Other LAN Gateways

The 3172 was designed to be a multiprotocol device and supports the Link layer and Network layer, which the older version of the 3745 did not support. The Link Layer protocol support includes Token Ring, FDDI, Ethernet, and ATM protocols. In addition, wide-area frame relay connections have also been added. On the channel side, the 3172 also supports Bus and Tag and ESCON. While it has native SNA support, it also was the first device to support native IP access to the mainframe. Channel attached routers are clones of 3172s when considering a mainframe attachment. Their mainframe configuration to support both SNA and TCP is identical to the 3172. These devices do a good job with all the protocols, but are as efficient in providing native SNA support as a front-end processor. However, they can be a more cost-effective solution than FEPs.

The 3174 controller is typically thought of as the ability to connect 3270 coax terminals to the mainframe and also provide channel gateway support. Support is provided to devices connected to Ethernet and Token Ring LANs. The 3174 is a very fast processor and efficiently supports native SNA traffic into the mainframe. However the 3174 has several issues, including redundancy, ease of configuration, and maintainability. These concerns have not made the 3174 the most desirable choice for channel connections.

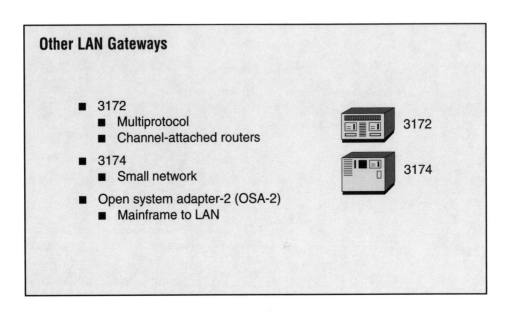

Other LAN Gateways

- 3172
  - Multiprotocol
  - Channel-attached routers   3172
- 3174
  - Small network   3174
- Open system adapter-2 (OSA-2)
  - Mainframe to LAN

IBM also has an Open Systems Adapter, or Open Systems Adapter 2 (OSA-2), which provides native LAN connection in the form of Ethernet, Token Ring, and ATM directly to the IBM mainframe. The OSA-2 adapter can render the other channel connections obsolete as it currently supports both TCP/IP and legacy SNA traffic over its ethernet and token ring interfaces. This is a very low cost solution, and early reports show it to be a excellent performer. The ATM adapters support only TCP/IP and APPN using VTAM version 4.4.

60 LAN Interfaces

LAN Interfaces

- IBM communications controllers
    - 3746 model 900 or 950 (16/4)
        - TIC 3
    - 3745 (16/4)
        - TIC 1 (old and poor performance 4 MB only)
        - TIC 2 (most popular type 16/4 MB)
    - 3725, 3720 (4)
    - 3705 (none)

- IBM cluster controller/control unit
    - 3174 (16/4 or 4)
    - 3274 (none)

IBM 3745 has an attachment model called a 3746, model 900, or a 3746, model 950. The 950 version is a standalone APPN or IP router that does not use a 3745 base. In any case, the LAN interfaces on these technologies include a high-performance Token Ring interface coupler (TIC3) for the 3746. The 3745 supports two types of TICs: The first is a TIC1, which only supports 4 megabits. The TIC2 is much more popular and supports both 16- and 4-megabit Token Ring adapters. The TIC2 has very good performance. Older devices, such as the 3725 and the 3720, support only TIC1. The oldest device, 3705, has no LAN support. The IBM 3174 control units support both the TIC1 and TIC2 connections. The oldest controller, the 3274, does not support any Token Ring interfaces.

Controller Positioning

The various SNA channel-attached devices can be viewed as "NIC" (network interface card) for your mainframe. Earlier we discussed a network-centric environment in which all devices are peers. The mainframe position in this environment is one as an application server to support traditional SNA along with newer TCP applications. This positions the mainframe as a *superserver* for your network. Considering this position, a channel gateway functions as a NIC to interface your server to its network clients. Now let's look at which NIC card is best for your environment.

There are various performance, configuration, maintenance, and cost considerations when selecting a gateway. Typically, you can consider these scaling from low (3174) to medium (3172) to highest (3745). There are, of course, exceptions. If you consider the size of your SNA network when selecting a gateway, make sure to consider SNA PUs as the primary measurement of a network's size.

A 3174 is typically used for smaller networks in which maximum physical unit support is limited to below 250 devices. 3172 would be for small- or medium-sized networks; while it supports more physical units than the 3174, its SNA throughput is not going to be as good as a 3745. The 3745 should be considered for both small and large networks. The base price of the 3745, before you pay reoccurring software charges, starts at just under $40,000.

Controller Positioning

- Position SNA channel gateway as mainframe "NIC" card
  - Network-centric environment
  - Mainframe is the superserver
- Gateway based on network size
  - Physical units
- IBM's high-performance channel gateways
  - 3174: Small to medium networks
  - 3172: Multiprotocol, small to medium networks
  - 3745: Small to very large networks, highest performance
  - 3746/950: APPN/ATM router

3174

3172

3745

This price includes two Token Ring connections and a Channel adapter. The 3745 can also be very expensive (over $1 million) and supports the largest LAN environments with the highest SNA performance. The 3746 model 950 is also a very high-performance box, but is limited to APPN and IP environments. It can be considered an APPN/ATM native SNA router connection for your enterprise.

Token Ring 62

```
Token Ring

■ Leading LAN technology in IBM
  networks
    ■ Standardized with 802.5 ISO 8805
    ■ Developed for LAN client/server
      applications (netbios)

■ Characteristics
    ■ Deterministic performance
    ■ Token passing
    ■ Initially used with shielded twisted
      pair (STP)
    ■ 4 MB or 16 MB per second
```

Token Ring is clearly the leading LAN technology used in SNA networks. It was standardized by the CCITT with the 802.5 specification and by the ISO standard 8805, and was initially used to support LAN client/server applications. Its outstanding characteristic is *deterministic performance* based on the token passing technology, because every workstation has the capability to transmit information between itself and its server. As a token is passed between each workstation on the ring, each workstation has that opportunity to attach data to the information and send it to its client. The token is released to the next workstation, only after it is finished sending a single frame.

Token Ring was initially developed with Shielded Twisted Pair technology, or STP, simply because it was believed that the laws of physics would never allow 16-megabits or higher transports to use Unshielded Twisted Pair (UTP). We know how the laws of physics may change from year to year, so today, UTP is the most popular media choice for Token Ring. Token Ring now supports 4 and 16 megabits per second with the standards bodies exploring higher-speed token packets at 100 or 128 megabits. Stay tuned and we will see how these new standards evolve.

Token Ring Session Setup, Discovery

How does SNA use Token Ring to set up sessions? It is a simple technique and let's look at it in greater detail. A workstation attempts to start a session by sending a TEST or XID frame to locate the MAC address of a session partner. This broadcast can take one of two forms: a single-route broadcast or an all-routes broadcast. A single-route broadcast is passed over a specific bridge pair, so if you have bridges in parallel between a source and a destination workstation, only a single path will be used. Single-route broadcasts are used to reduce the amount of broadcast that a network experiences. It also uses a Spanning Tree protocol, which determines the path for a single-route broadcast. An all-routes broadcast is a broadcast that is sent by all parallel bridges

between the destination and source workstations. This can cause significantly more broadcast traffic in your network.

The receiving device responds to all broadcasts it receives; however, the type of response differs based on whether an all-route or single-route broadcast was received. Let's look at the single-route broadcast first. As a single-route broadcast is propagated from a requesting workstation to its destination workstation, a defined set of bridges within this network forwards the single-route broadcast. However, when the destination workstation receives the single-route broadcast, it issues an all-routes broadcast, flooding the entire network with all available paths back to the originating work-

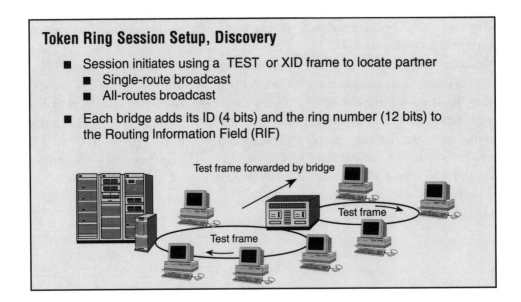

Token Ring Session Setup, Discovery

- Session initiates using a TEST or XID frame to locate partner
  - Single-route broadcast
  - All-routes broadcast
- Each bridge adds its ID (4 bits) and the ring number (12 bits) to the Routing Information Field (RIF)

Test frame forwarded by bridge

Test frame

Test frame

station. This may result in the originating workstation receiving multiple broadcasts back. The originating device uses the first broadcast it receives, guaranteeing the lowest-latency path between the two workstations.

An all-routes broadcast results when the workstation sends an all-routes broadcast to its destination. This may generate multiple paths to the originating workstation based on the network topology. The target workstation responds to each broadcast by sending a specifically routed frame back to the originating workstation. This can obviously generate more broadcasts than a single-route broadcast. The generating or requesting workstation uses the first acknowledgment it receives from the destination. It is important to note that a single-route broadcast environment reduces the broadcast by approximately half, but it does not eliminate all the broadcasts, since the destination workstation will issue an all-routes broadcast back. Therefore, the target device floods the network with broadcasts.

As the broadcast frame is forwarded by each bridge, the bridge adds a unique entry into the Routing Information Field (RIF). Each RIF entry is 16 bits long and includes 4 bits of bridge ID, which can range from hexadecimal 0 to F. The unique Token Ring number occupies the remaining 12 bits. A ring number can be in the range of hexadecimal 0 to FFF. The entire Routing Information field can have up to seven bridge and ring numbers. In addition to these 14 bytes, the RIF field contains 2 bytes of control information. When the RIF field is present, an additional 16 bytes (2 bytes of control and 14 bytes for RIF entries) of overhead can be added to the size of the Token Ring MAC frame. The 14 bytes are based on supporting 7 *hops* (bridges) between workstations.

When a broadcast MAC frame is received by the workstation, the workstation sends back a positive response. One response is sent per frame, except for single-route broadcasts in which an all-routes broadcast is used. Both session partners store the first entry that is used, including the RIF field, in cache, providing a unique path through the network. Each subsequent transmission uses a specifically routed frame based on the stored RIF information. This continues until the session is terminated by one of the devices. SRB guarantees that traffic will always take the most efficient path between the communicating devices. Also, broadcasts are not used until the session is taken down and another one is started up.

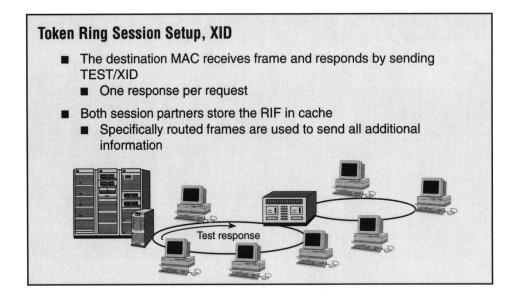

Token Ring Session Setup, XID

- The destination MAC receives frame and responds by sending TEST/XID
  - One response per request
- Both session partners store the RIF in cache
  - Specifically routed frames are used to send all additional information

Test response

Logical Link Control (LLC)

Logical Link Control (LLC)

- Logical Link Control (LLC)
  - Controls how information flows between LAN-attached devices
  - 802.2 SAPs/control fields
    - LLC1: Connectionless
    - LLC2: Connection

As we discussed earlier, Logical Link Control 2, or LLC2, controls how information between LAN-attached devices is transmitted. We also identified the two types of Logical Link Control: LLC1 and LLC2. Remember that LLC1 is connectionless and used by IP. IP relies on higher-level protocols to perform error correction and retransmission.

SNA traffic uses connection protocols at layer 2. LLC2 is used by SNA LAN devices to provide the reliable delivery of information. SNA does not need higher-layer protocols to perform error detection and data retransmission; this is handled by LLC2. LLC2 provides this function by synchronizing send and receive counts within the LLC2 datagram.

66 LLC2

As a connection-oriented protocol, LLC2 provides local acknowledgments based on a predetermined window size. The LLC2 is used to encapsulate SNA for both Token Ring and Ethernet networks. Note that LLC2 as defined in the 802.2 spec is not limited to Token Ring networks. It is also used to transport SNA traffic in Ethernet environments. LLC2 uses pool frames based on time intervals described earlier (T1 and Ti) to ensure that traffic is transmitted between workstations and that the workstations remain within sessions.

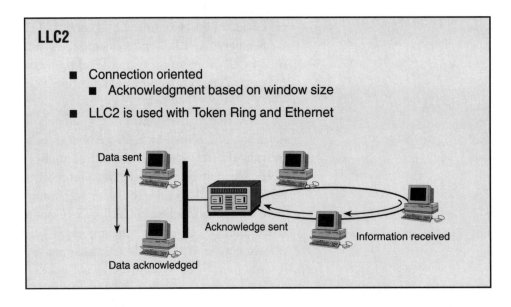

LLC2

■ Connection oriented
  ■ Acknowledgment based on window size
■ LLC2 is used with Token Ring and Ethernet

Data sent

Acknowledge sent

Data acknowledged

Information received

LLC2 Timers, T1

An SNA session is required between two devices before communications can occur. After the session is established, each device needs to constantly verify that its session partner is still working. Keep-alive LLC2 poll frames (Receiver/Ready, RR) are transmitted at configured intervals. In addition, any time information is transmitted between the two session partners, an RR poll is used by LLC2 to verify that the information is received. The RR poll is sent out after a configured number of frames are sent or when the transmitting device has nothing else to send. The frame count is referred to as *window size* and is typically set to 2 in most LLC2 default configurations. This means two frames can be sent before an acknowledgment is required.

The T1 timer starts when a session sends information to a destination or a server. This timer is usually hard-coded and not able to be changed by the user (it is normally set to one and one-half seconds). If a response is not received before the T1 timer expires, an error recovery is initiated on these devices. If error recovery fails, or a device goes into error recovery, the SNA session may fail and try to restart. This requires that the partners restart their sessions, and users log back on and restart their application.

The RR-acknowledged polls were designed to act on a high-bandwidth LAN; the bandwidth available on LANs typically can support the "chattiness" of LLC2. However, as LANs

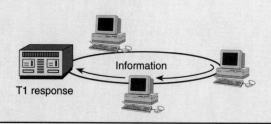

LLC2 Timers, T1

- Devices in session are constantly communicating to ensure session partner is active

- T1 (response) timer
    - Starts when a station sends information
    - If no response before T1 expires, error recovery is initiated
    - Difficult to determine in WANs

Information

T1 response

grow and are networked together with bridges and then slow, wide-area connections, LLC2 devices encounter numerous issues. This is a result of the limited bandwidth across wide-area connections. The LLC2 timers can easily expire before the RR acknowledge from a partner station is received. This problem is magnified when different types of information and protocols are also using these limited network resources; for example, mixing the small SNA frame sizes with IP file transfer or large Web browser applications. T1 timers can easily expire before the acknowledgment is received, resulting in session failures.

Receiver/Ready (RR) polls are used to determine whether SNA devices are still in session. The end devices include configuration parameters on how often the RR polls are sent and how quickly a poll must be acknowledged.

The Ti Inactivity, or *keep-alive*, timer is used with the RR poll to ensure the session partner is still available. It is sent after a period of idle time (Ti), which may be several seconds or minutes. This idle period starts when the last frame was either sent or received by a station. Note that constant information exchange may result in the Ti timer never expiring. If the timer expires, an RR is sent to the session partner to ensure that the partner is still active. The length of the LLC2 packet is based on the LAN's MAC frame. In a Token Ring network, the LLC2 packet can be between 25–43 bytes long, based on the number of bridges and the size of the RIF field. You can see how this can add additional network overhead.

Typically, the Ti value is coded by the end user; however, it is sometimes hard-coded by software, making it inaccessible to tuning. Also note that both stations have Ti timers. This may result in difficulty in troubleshooting and tuning your SNA network. For example, if one station sends an RR poll every 60 seconds and its partner is configured to send a poll every 10 seconds, the station with the timer set for 60 seconds will never expire. This is because there will always be traffic between

LLC2 Timers, Ti
- Ti (inactivity or "keep-alive") timer
  - Sent after an idle period
  - Generates a Receiver Ready to the session partner
    - Ensures partner is still there
  - A Receiver Ready is 25 to 43 bytes
    - Variable size based on length of the RIF field
  - May be user coded or "hard coded" by software

T1 timer
T1 timer
T1 response

these devices. This can make LLC2 difficult to tune within your network. Setting a higher-response timer at a server or on a gateway device does not necessarily ensure that each of its remote devices will be send Inactivity polls within the configured (Ti) span of time. The remote devices may have much shorter Ti timers, and the Ti timer and the RR polls they generate can produce a significant amount of traffic across the network.

LLC2 Timers, T2 69

The T2 acknowledgment timer is an LLC2 timer that was developed to help control the amount of RR polls that are sent across the network. It delays sending an acknowledgment based on the number of received frames and a timer value (T2). As frames are received, a time-out counter is started. The receiving station does not respond to each frame, but rather waits for the counter to reach its limit or for the timer to expire.

The T2 timer is typically user defined. It can generate many problems in the network if not tuned correctly. I typically recommend that the T2 timer be left alone.

70

SNA Activation,
SDLC Switched Line

SNA LAN-attached PUs are activated using dial (switched-line) protocols. This is very similar to the activation of a PU on an SDLC wide-area line. You can see in the slide that an XID is sent from the front-end processor to the remote workstation. After that, an SNRM (Set Normal Response Mode) is sent to initialize the Send and Receive counts. A positive response is sent from the receiving device, using the SDLC command UA (Unnumbered Acknowledgment). The link activation continues by sending the SNA commands to activate the physical and logical units between the host and that workstation.

It is important to note that the SDLC switched connection is not what is typically used on an SDLC line. The typical SDLC line is a leased, dedicated facility provided by the phone company and is attached directly to a front-end processor.

SNA LAN technology is based on using this SDLC dial startup procedure. The next slide illustrates the activation of a LAN device.

SNA Activation, SDLC Switched Line

3745   3174

- Activation is based on switched (dial) connection

  SDLC switched line

  Note: Most lines connected to the 3745 are *nonswitched* (no XIDs are exchanged)

- XID identifies incoming or calling device

- Set Normal Response Mode (SNRM)
  - Initializes link-level (SDLC) send/receive counts

XID — — — — — →
← — — — — — XID (+RSP)
SNRM — — — — — →
← — — — — — UA
ACTPU — — — — — →
← — — — — — ACTPU(+RSP)
ACTLU — — — — — →
← — — — — — ACTLU(+RSP)

SNA Activation, LAN (LLC2) Connection

An SABME (Set Asynchronous Balanced Mode Extended) replaces the SNRM. The SABME is used to initialize the Send and Receive counts of the LLC2 frame. In the previous slide, we saw that the SNRM, or Set Normal Response Mode, initialized the Send and Receive counts of the SDLC frame. So, functionally, these have the same meaning. An unnumbered acknowledgment is received from the remote device confirming the SABME command and initializes the device's Send and Receive counts. This is flowed by the SNA commands to activate the physical and logical units.

Note that SNA LAN technology is similar to, and based on, older protocols that were used for SDLC dial connections.

SNA Activation, LAN (LLC2) Connection

■ Activation is based on switched (dial) connection

■ Broadcast for MAC address is added (test frame)

■ Set Asynchronous Balanced Mode Extended (SABME) replaces SNRM
   ■ Initializes LLC Send/Receive counts

```
            Gateway                  PU
          ┌─────────────────────┐
          │     LAN attached     │
          └─────────────────────┘
          Note: SABME replaces SNRM

                  ← — — — — — TEST
          TEST — — — — — →
                  ← — — — — — XID (null)
          XID — — — — — →
                  ← — — — — — XID (+RSP)
          SABME — — — — — →
                  ← — — — — — UA
          ACTPU — — — — — →
                  ← — — — — — ACTPU(+RSP)
          ACTLU — — — — — →
                  ← — — — — — ACTLU(+RSP)
```

Summary: SNA Limitations

Summary: SNA Limitations

- LLC2 issues
  - Assumes reliable delivery

- SRB issues
  - Broadcasts
  - No reroutability
  - Maximum of 7 hops
  - Unique ring numbers required
  - Session time-outs
    - T1 and T1 timeouts

We have identified several issues in this Part that I want to review before we continue. LLC2 is the LAN protocol that provides reliable and connection-oriented services that SNA requires. It ensures reliable delivery by sequencing on Send and Receive frame counts and uses RR polls and timer values (Ti and T1) to ensure that traffic is transmitted or session partners are still active. In congested or busy networks, the LLC2 timers may either be dropped or delayed to avoid SNA session outages.

Source route bridging, one of the most popular early LAN integration technologies, presents several problems. It is broadcast intensive, and it can not reroute around failed links or bridges. It is also limited to the amount of hops (bridge and ring pairs) that can exist between devices. This will limit the topology of the network since devices cannot have more than 7 hops between them.

These problems challenge the network designer and manager to provide reliable and predictable communications for SNA users. The next Part overviews the various solutions that can be used to simplify your network and support SNA.

Part Seven

SNA Integration Technologies

SNA Integration
Solutions Overview

In this Part, we will discuss the various integration solutions within the enterprise. This includes source route bridging (which we have already touched upon), IP encapsulation and sync pass-Through, Datalink Switching, (DLSw), RFC 1490, and APPN. In addition, several gateway technologies are emerging as popular solutions for SNA. These include TN3270, TN3270E, and Web browser access to the mainframe.

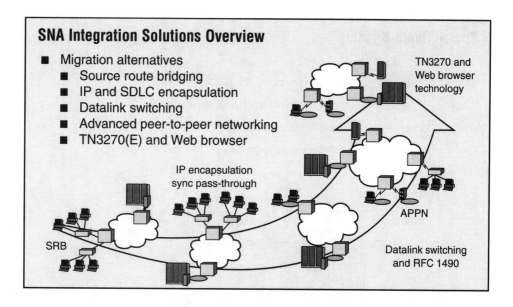

SNA Integration Solutions Overview

■ Migration alternatives
   ■ Source route bridging
   ■ IP and SDLC encapsulation
   ■ Datalink switching
   ■ Advanced peer-to-peer networking
   ■ TN3270(E) and Web browser

TN3270 and Web browser technology

IP encapsulation sync pass-through

APPN

SRB

Datalink switching and RFC 1490

74. Source Route Bridging

Source route bridging is a layer 2 protocol and was originally the entry point of LAN integration for SNA traffic. Its characteristics include dynamic discovery of endstations and routes, which we covered in detail previously in Part Six. This discovery aids SNA in providing flexible LAN designs. The RIF (Routing Information protocol) field is added to the Token Ring MAC headers during this dynamic discovery. There are no routing tables or MAC addresses to maintain in the bridges. The RIFs are stored in the endstations, so after a device is discovered, the most efficient path is learned. This path is used to send data between the partners for the entire session.

Source route bridging has the best forwarding performance of any of the SNA integration technologies. This is because bridge technology, whether it is in source route bridging or other technologies such as transparent bridging or learning bridge, produces the simplest and shortest program path to process packets. Traffic entering on one interface is quickly forwarded to another interface. The Token Ring endstations use LLC2 for reliable delivery of traffic. We discussed the characteristics and the potential problems with LLC2 in Part Six.

Source Route Bridging

- Original LAN entry point for SNA
- Dynamic discovery of endstations and routes
- High forwarding performance
- Uses LLC2 for reliable delivery

Source route bridging is limited to 7 hops or 7 bridge and ring numbers. Source route bridging is subject to multiple broadcast storms because Token Ring endstations are discovered via a broadcast mechanism. For example, consider two remote locations: one with a remote workstation, the other with an SNA host. The remote device initiates a session with the host by issuing a all-routes broadcast. The broadcast is forwarded across the bridge and put on the local ring. Since the broadcast contains the MAC address of the host, when the host receives it, a response is sent back to the broadcasting device. The path is known, since the source route bridges built an RIF field and inserted the ring and bridge numbers used along the transmission path.

This is a very simple example in establishing a session with an SNA host. The single broadcast over a single bridge does not generate any significant overhead. This is because our example includes only one bridge and two locations. Now imagine 199 other locations, giving us a total of 200 locations connected to the same SNA host. Each remote ring is connected with two bridges (one for redundancy). Note that SRB can have parallel active bridges between LANs. When one workstation wants to send and broadcast to the host, it is forwarded to the local ring over both bridges, doubling our broadcasts. Additionally, the other 398 bridges (primary and backup) process the broadcast and propagate it to 199 other remotes. As we add workstations, more

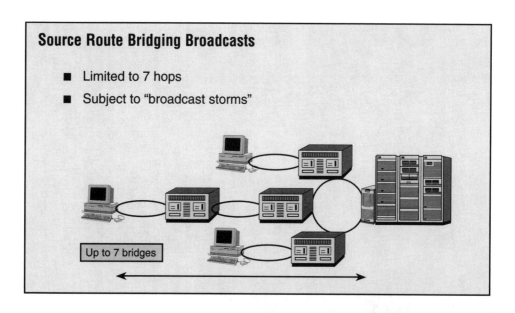

Source Route Bridging Broadcasts

- Limited to 7 hops
- Subject to "broadcast storms"

Up to 7 bridges

broadcasts are generated. This can result in broadcast storms that can gobble up the precious wide-area bandwidth and can affect bridges and servers, since each Token Ring device needs to process every broadcast.

The other issue with source route bridging is based in the chipset that is used. Multiport bridges, which today are routers supporting bridges on multiple ports, have to implement an internal ring number. That is, simply because the way the chipsets are designed, you need to pass information from one ring, into a bridge, and into another ring. On a multiport bridge, it would be impossible to take data off of one interface and then pass it to all the other interfaces. So, what typically is implemented is an internal ring. This allows all the traffic to be forwarded to the internal ring and then bridged out to each of the individual interfaces.

So what's the big deal? Remember, the RIF field is limited to 7 ring and bridge counts.

The internal ring counts as a ring and bridge hop. So, going through a multiport bridge can dramatically reduce your bridge hop counts, as every bridge counts as two entries in the RIF field. This can dramatically affect the design of your network, limiting it to as few as two multiport bridge hops between devices. The good news is that there have been many router/bridge implementations that reduce the internal ring numbers. So, it may not be a problem based on which vendor's equipment you use.

You should still consider source route bridging as a good solution for many customers. This is especially true for smaller networks with a moderate number of workstations. Its topology

Enhanced Source Route Bridging

- Multiport bridge
  - Internal ring number
  - All routers count as 1 hop
- Still a valid solution for many customers (moderate number of stations, simple topology)

Multiport bridge

and implementation are very simple. Based on what you are trying to accomplish and the amount of protocols that you require in your network, it still may be a valid SNA solution.

SDLC Encapsulation

SDLC encapsulation, as the name implies, is the ability to take an SDLC frame and encapsulate it in another protocol; typically, UDP/IP or a MAC frame is used to encapsulate the SDLC frame. Originally, there was no packet acknowledgment or termination of the packet, which resulted in many of the time-sensitive polls being transmitted across the WAN. Also, because SDLC polls are very time sensitive, if routers became delayed or dropped packets, there was no recovery mechanism, so these SDLC polls could be lost. As SDLC polls are lost, workstations go into recovery and devices can lose sessions. Typical implementations do not support multidrop lines that are very popular in SNA designs. In the earlier SDLC example we discussed a multidrop line connecting a New York data center with remote devices in Washington, DC, Raleigh, and Atlanta. If we were to convert the SDLC lines and use routers and SDLC encapsulation, we would need to install three point-to-point lines between the remote routers and the central site data center. (This can be a frame relay network.) Each remote router would have a point-to-point SDLC connection to the SNA controllers. The SNA SDLC frames would be encapsulated and sent to the central site routers. The central site router would need three point-to-point lines that connect to the front-end processor. This would increase the ports required on the FEP, which would be a very expensive upgrade.

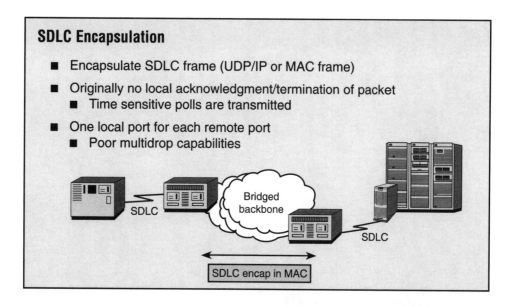

SDLC Encapsulation

- Encapsulate SDLC frame (UDP/IP or MAC frame)
- Originally no local acknowledgment/termination of packet
  - Time sensitive polls are transmitted
- One local port for each remote port
  - Poor multidrop capabilities

SDLC

Bridged backbone

SDLC

SDLC encap in MAC

SDLC encapsulation does a poor job of supporting multidrop SDLC lines over an intranet. Despite these problems, this technology can still be considered for systems that need to reduce expenses and do not have any LAN-attached devices to the mainframe. Although not robust, SDLC encapsulation does provide a solution to users migrating from SNA host who do not want to spend the time and money to upgrade the FEP to LAN technology.

IP Encapsulation

IP encapsulation is very similar to SDLC encapsulation. IP encapsulation takes an entire Token Ring MAC frame and encapsulates it in an IP packet. UDP is typically used as the layer 4 transport protocol. UDP is simple to implement, but is a connectionless protocol. IP encapsulation has several advantages over the SRB environment. First, it significantly reduces the amount of broadcasts within the network. This is a result of not having SRB configured on wide-area connections. Broadcasts are specially directed between LANs. It also reduces the size of the RIF field, since the entire IP backbone appears as a single hop. The IP backbone takes up a single entry in the RIF field, reducing the number of hops that could physically be crossed and also

the number of bytes carried in the MAC frame. In addition, IP provides the capability to route packets around failed routers or links. Remember that SRB does not support rerouting traffic. Source route bridging uses a RIF that specifically defines the path between the two stations in the network. If one of the components in that path fails, the session terminates because the packet is not deliverable.

A caution on rerouting of SNA packets: SNA devices use LLC2 RR to ensure data is transmitted and the partner station is still active. After an RR or poll is sent, a timer starts (T1 or Ti). The network takes time to converge around a failed facility. Often this time is much longer that the time-out values

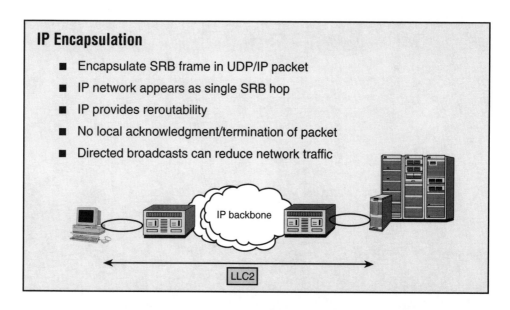

IP Encapsulation

- Encapsulate SRB frame in UDP/IP packet
- IP network appears as single SRB hop
- IP provides reroutability
- No local acknowledgment/termination of packet
- Directed broadcasts can reduce network traffic

IP backbone

LLC2

needed by LLC2, so you will need to optimize both the IP network and the SNA network to ensure the sessions do not time-out while the network is converging. Typically, most networks take several minutes to converge, which is normally unacceptable in an SNA environment. A carefully tuned OSPF network may take as little as 10 or 15 seconds to converge and reroute, which may be an acceptable time to keep SNA sessions active, making an OSPF a better protocol to use in order to maintain SNA session integrity.

IP encapsulation does have several problems. First, it does not provide local acknowledgment or termination of the packets (LLC2 RR polls) on either side of the network. This causes all LLC2 traffic to cross the network, generating additional overhead. More importantly, packets are subject to being dropped or delayed, which results in increased traffic, unreliable delivery of SNA packets, and lost sessions.

Now let's discuss in detail the benefits of DLSw, and examine how DLSw reliably transports SNA traffic across the IP enterprise environment.

DLSw was designed to ensure reliable integration of SNA traffic across multiprotocol networks. Multiprotocol networks today are built using routers to support IP and IPX. Sometimes other protocols such as Banyon Vines, AppleTalk or DecNet, are required; however, these protocols are decreasing in popularity as many systems are being migrated to IP-based systems. The enterprise supported two parallel networks, one for the router traffic and the other to support the legacy SNA systems. This became very expensive to support and maintain. We have just explored the various techniques used to integrate SNA into this multiprotocol environment. We will now take a closer look at DLSw in order to understand its technology and advantages and why it is probably the best integration technique for migrating SNA into your enterprise environment.

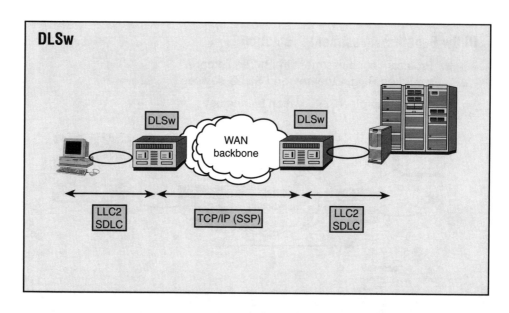

80 DLSw Benefits: Investment Protection

DLSw was originally designed to protect the investment in IBM hardware and software; specifically, Token Ring and SDLC-attached devices, along with the 3270 SNA mainframe applications. Ethernet and FDDI are also supported, along with other protocols such as ATM. Since most SNA devices were connected to either Token Ring or SDLC networks, DLSw was initially designed for those environments. That is why we discussed Token Ring and LLC2 earlier. This technology was critical to the development of DLSw. It is important to obtain an understanding of Token Ring and LLC2 technology and the problems they create. Now we can see how DLSw solves them.

I refer to DLSw as the best multiprotocol integration technology. That is a very subjective statement and is based on a lot of experience within the industry. It solves issues that are apparent in IP and SDLC encapsulation and source route bridging. While it may not be as robust as APPN (we will discuss APPN later in this Part), it does provide the capability to support SNA. It accomplishes this by following a series of RFCs and standards that are accepted in the industry. To better understand the benefits of DLSw versus APPN, let's use a BETA/VHS analogy. Where BETA was clearly a better technology choice, VHS became a more popular mechanism to view and record videos. So, in this case, the better technology

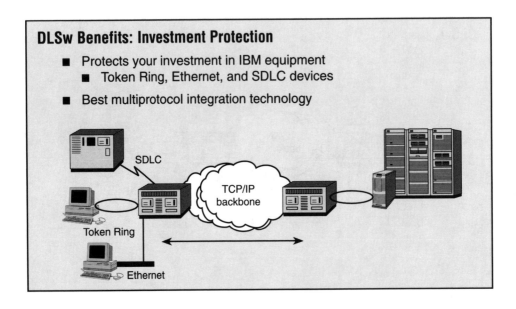

DLSw Benefits: Investment Protection

- Protects your investment in IBM equipment
  - Token Ring, Ethernet, and SDLC devices
- Best multiprotocol integration technology

lost. APPN is arguably one of the better technologies available but has lost user acceptance to prevalent TCP/IP technology.

DLSw was first defined in RFC 1434 and as you will see later, there are other RFCs, specifically 1735 and 2166, that provide additional documentation and enhancements to the original RFC.

81

DLSw Benefits: Enhanced WAN Access

Any SNA integration technology must provide the SNA customer with a reliable, available, and predictable level of performance. DLSw accomplishes this by enveloping SNA datagrams in a TCP/IP frame. TCP provides the reliability required in many SNA applications. IP provides a resilient and robust routing ability to quickly forward packets and find alternate routes if a link or node fails. Integrating multiprotocol traffic with SNA runs several risks. First, there is no way to provide end-to-end Class of Service routing within IP. This puts SNA performance in jeopardy. Second, mixing unpredictable multiprotocol traffic with SNA can cause SNA packets to be starved of critical network resources. While there is no guarantee this will occur, the router and network design offer some major relief. Typically, SNA networks run on slow, multidrop lines. When router networks are installed they typically use high-speed, point-to-point lines. This additional bandwidth substantially improves the performance of the SNA network. In addition, routers offer various priority schemes that allow you to configure SNA as the top priority exiting the router.

DLSw inherently provides protocol conversion for SNA. It has the ability to take frames that originated on Token Ring, Ethernet, SDLC, frame relay, or any other layer 2 interface; and transmit only the SNA portion (SNA TH/RH/RU) across the enterprise network; and deliver it to any layer 2

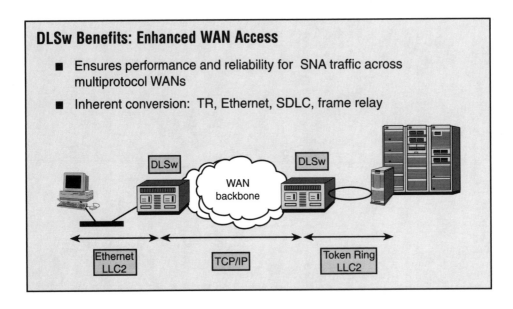

DLSw Benefits: Enhanced WAN Access

- ■ Ensures performance and reliability for SNA traffic across multiprotocol WANs

- ■ Inherent conversion: TR, Ethernet, SDLC, frame relay

interface. It does this because the interface rebuilds the layer 2 frame. The most common example is a remote device that is Ethernet or SDLC attached and connects to the central site mainframe using a Token Ring-attached gateway.

82 DLSw Benefits: Scaling and Interoperability

DLSw can scale to support very large networks. It has been improved with updated RFCs that specifically address performance and scalability of DLSw. These improvements include features that reduce TCP sessions, eliminate sessions that are inactive, and provide capabilities exchange that allow routers to understand the version of DLSw that can be supported and its associated features. Specific flow control methods are also described, which the routers will implement to support SNA.

Although DLSw was designed to scale to very large networks, initially it did not do that very well. There are various reasons for this, but none greater than code immaturity. As new technology is introduced, bugs must be worked out in the corresponding software. Along with waiting for the code to mature, the available processing power and memory capabilities of routers were limited. When DLSw was introduced, most router technology was based on 286 or 386 Intel processors or their equivalents and 4 and 8 megabytes of memory. Today's largest routers exceed 800 megabytes of memory and have routing processors based on high-speed RISC or Pentium 2 technology.

DLSw is based on standards defined in the TCP/IP community as Request For Comments (RFCs). However, not every RFC becomes a standard. The first DLSw RFC 1434 was never standardized; however, almost every router vendor supported it. It quickly become a *de*

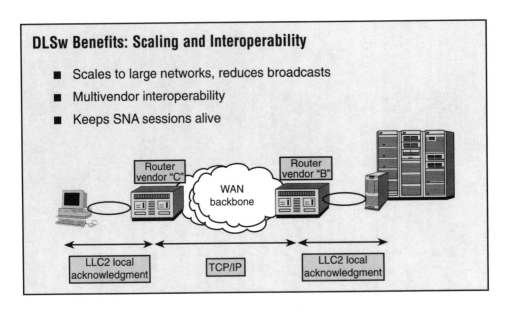

DLSw Benefits: Scaling and Interoperability

- Scales to large networks, reduces broadcasts
- Multivendor interoperability
- Keeps SNA sessions alive

facto standard. (An RFC becomes a standard when the InterNet Engineers Task Force, (IETF) meets and votes to approve the RFC as a standard.) The more recent DLSw RFCs (1735 and 2166) have been voted on and approved by the IETF, thereby making them standards. These RFCs are known as DLSw Version 1 (RFC 1795) and DLSw Version 2 (RFC 2166). We will review the differences in the RFCs later. Together, these RFCs combine to provide multivendor interoperability. So, regardless of which router vendor(s) you select, you should be able to build an enterprise integrated SNA network that interoperates.

One of the most important features of DLSw is the ability to support local acknowledgment of LLC2 RR and SDLC polls. Remember from our earlier LLC2 and SDLC discussions that LLC2 and SDLC polls are very time sensitive. If the proper acknowledgment is not received before the LLC2 T1 or Ti timer expires or missed SDLC polls, the SNA session can be disrupted. Local acknowledgment ensures that these polls are *not* transmitted across the WAN, so SNA session disruption because of missed polls is eliminated.

DLSw Benefits: SNA Routing

DLSw Benefits: SNA Routing

- Offload FEP: FEP does not make routing decisions
  - Network centric: Hosts a big superserver

- Seamless rerouting (even outside of frame relay cloud)
  - Dial backup

- DLSw prioritizaition
  - Multiprotocol and SNA prioritization

DLSw also offloads the FEP from participating in the router network. Earlier we discussed the host-centric environment and saw that the FEP was the center of the legacy network. The disadvantage with this solution was, when the mainframe went down, so did the network. In today's multivendor and server environment, the enterprise cannot afford the loss of the network due to the failure of an application server. The mainframe is positioned as a big superserver in the network-centric environment. The router "front ends" the mainframe along with all the enterprise servers, so a server or mainframe failure has no effect on the network. DLSw also provides seamless rerouting. Dial backup or meshed network designs provide solutions to transport SNA traffic around failed network resources.

Since IP is used, alternate paths can be found before an SNA session outage occurs. IP can reroute around the failed facility, and DLSw local acknowledgments ensure the SNA will not fail.

DLSw also provides, at least in most vendor implementations, the ability to give SNA a higher priority than other traffic existing on the router. This is not part of the RFC, but rather a vendor extension that does not inhibit interoperability. DLSw prioritization can ensure that the most important SNA traffic is transmitted before other protocol traffic and less important SNA traffic. This provides a method with which to improve your integrated SNA traffic. In fact, we will see many extensions to the DLSw standard that take advantage of router vendor's implementation and expand the robustness of the SNA integration. Every vendor has these "proprietary extensions," but some do a better job of marketing than others. Since these are locally implemented and vendor specific, you need to contact or understand how your vendor implements these techniques. Typically, DLSw's TCP ports provide a very simple way in which to implement priority filters.

84 DLSw: Explorer Broadcast Reduction

Datalink switching reduces bandwidth requirements and eliminates broadcasts across the network. In the example that you see here, we have a partially meshed environment. A remote SNA workstation wants to find its host, so it sends a broadcast frame. The router receives the broadcast on its LAN interface and then converts it to a specific DLSw command. The DLSw CANUREACH verb is used. The CANUREACH frame is specifically sent to routers that are configured as peers to the remote router. In the example you see, we have two rings that never receive this broadcast. The central site router receives the CANUREACH frame and floods a test frame with the destination's MAC address out all the DLSw interfaces. The host then responds back to the central site router, and the router responds with an ICANREACH frame, telling the remote router that it found the host. DLSw can dramatically reduce the broadcast by directing it to specific routers and then to specific interfaces. Note that the central site router will not flood the broadcast frame to non-DLSw configured interfaces. This example shows the flexibility in configuring DLSw. DLSw can communicate with every router in this diagram, but in most SNA environments, all the devices are talking to a central site mainframe. This makes it easier to configure, design, and maintain DLSw networks.

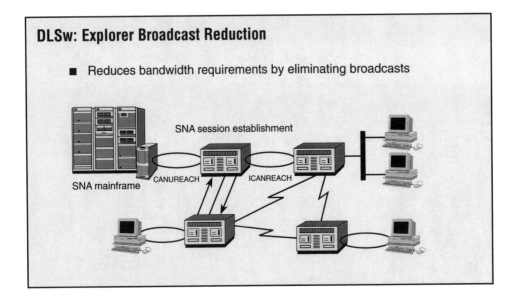

DLSw: Explorer Broadcast Reduction

■ Reduces bandwidth requirements by eliminating broadcasts

SNA session establishment

SNA mainframe   CANUREACH   ICANREACH

DLSw: Extended Source Route Bridging

85

DLSw spoofs the LLC2 session on each side of the network, and it also terminates the SRB RIF field. A device can be bridged to the remote or central site router with several hops. Since DLSw terminates the LLC2 session, the source route RIF is also terminated. This provides relief in configuring and building SRB networks. It allows duplicate ring numbers and more than seven rings and bridges between devices. For example, in an environment that has 500 remote Token Rings, each ring would need a unique ring number in a bridged environment. Since DLSw terminates the source route RIF and LLC2 session, each remote ring can be configured with the same ring number. This can make installation and configuration easier.

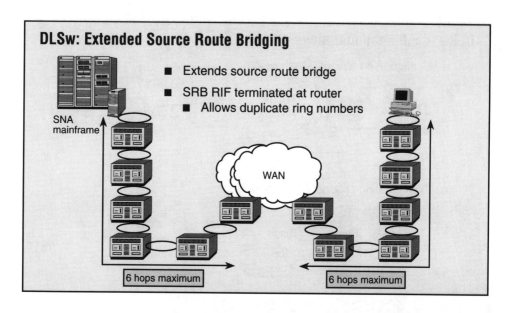

86

DLSw: Configuration Options

There are two basic configuration options with DLSw: *dual switch* and *single switch*. Dual switch, as the name implies, requires at least two routers. In a dual-switch environment, one router communicates over an IP network with another router. These environments are often designed as numerous remote routers communicating to a central site data center. The IP backbone can be a combination of routers and both LANs and WANs. A variety of link-level protocols can be used to connect these routers, since DLSw is unaware of these network links. These can include frame relay, leased line, SMDS, ATM, and dial access, to name some of the more popular protocol. Datalink switching is configured on the egress and ingress points of the network, where traffic is transmitted to and from the SNA workstations.

A single-switch environment consists of a single router. The router connects to the SNA interface and provides the ability to convert from one link-level protocol to another. The most common application for single-switch DLSw is to convert SDLC lines to Token Ring. Note that although the DLSw RFCs acknowledge this ability, they do not describe how this is accomplished. Almost every vendor who implements DLSw also provides this support.

Single-switch technology is the basis of RFC 1490 frame relay support. Boundary Network Node (BNN) and Boundary Access

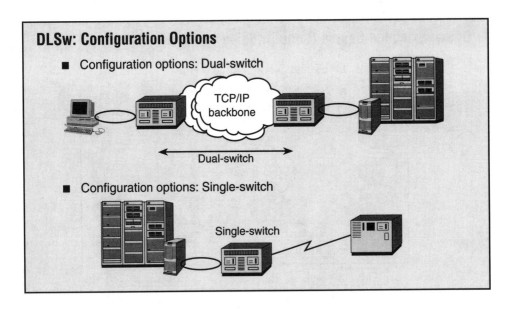

Node (BAN) technology provides the conversion of SDLC or LAN-attached devices to a frame relay format (this is covered in greater detail later in this Part). FEPs that can support frame relay can now connect to remote devices that are attached to either traditional routers or Frame Relay Access Devices (FRADs). The FEP can be migrated from the traditional SDLC WAN environment to support SNA over a router-attached network. As always, there are several issues with this method and we will discuss them in more detail later.

87

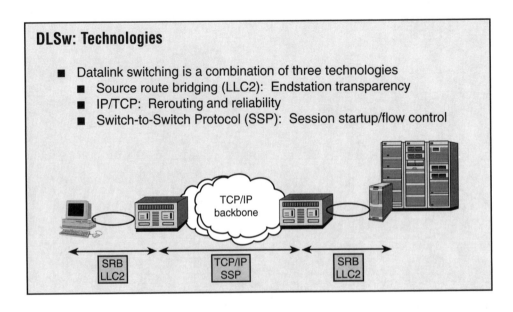

DLSw: Technologies

Datalink switching is built on four older technologies and a new protocol (Switch-to-Switch Protocol, or SSP) described in the DLSw RFCs. DLSw uses source route bridging (SRB) and LLC2, IP, and TCP technologies to form the basic interface and transport protocols to support SNA traffic. SRB was the original LAN integration technology for SNA. It is simple to implement, but uses LLC2, which causes problems when integrating with other protocols over a WAN. It also uses TCP/IP to provide rerouting across the network and the ability to find an alternate path if a network resource fails. TCP provides the reliability that SNA systems require. TCP guarantees that traffic is transmitted between endstations, assuring its packets are reassembled and received without any errors.

Source route bridging and TCP/IP are very mature technologies and result in very mature router code. When DLSw was first developed, router vendors were very familiar with these implementations. However, it is also based on a new protocol called Switch-to-Switch protocol (SSP). SSP defines all the DLSw session setup and termination techniques and flow controls that exist between the two routers.

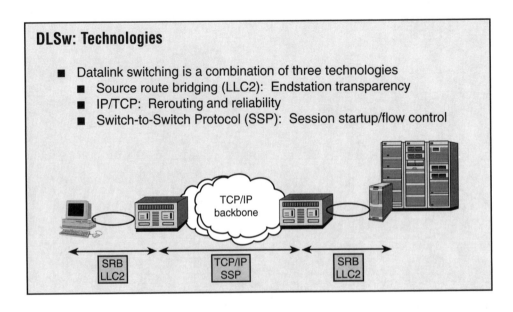

DLSw: Technologies

- ■ Datalink switching is a combination of three technologies
  - ■ Source route bridging (LLC2): Endstation transparency
  - ■ IP/TCP: Rerouting and reliability
  - ■ Switch-to-Switch Protocol (SSP): Session startup/flow control

| SRB | TCP/IP | SRB |
| LLC2 | SSP | LLC2 |

TCP/IP backbone

In order to illustrate DLSw technology, I am going to use a simple Token Ring example. We discussed LAN connections and LLC2 earlier, so you should be familiar with this technology. In this example, a remote Token Ring device will start a session to an SNA mainframe. Remember that although this example uses Token Ring, DLSw is not limited exclusively to Token Ring support. Ethernet, SDLC, FDDI, frame relay, and ATM are also supported.

A typical LAN session is initiated with a broadcast TEST frame. The TEST frame is sent by the workstation and received on the router's Token Ring interface. The router interface is typically configured with SRB. It appears to the workstation as a bridge and for-wards the SRB packet to the DLSw function within the router. The router's DLSw function converts the TEST frame to a specific SSP frame called the CANUREACH. The CANUREACH frame is directed to a DLSw peer configured within the router. In this example, you see that the CANUREACH is sent only to the router at the mainframe location. The other routers in the network do not receive that frame. When the central site router receives the CANUREACH frame, it converts it to a broadcast TEST frame and floods it out all the DLSw interfaces. When the destination device receives the broadcast (in this example, the FEP), it responds with a positive acknowledgment TEST frame. The central site router receives this frame and

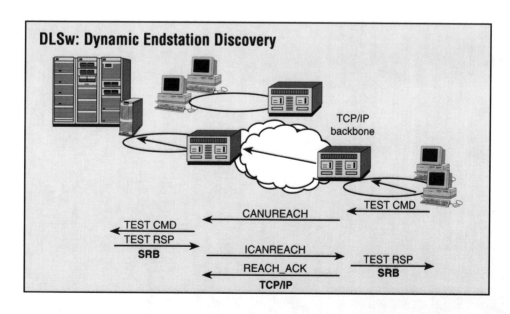

DLSw: Dynamic Endstation Discovery

converts the TEST response to an SSP ICANREACH frame and sends it to the originating remote router. When the ICAN-REACH frame is received by the originating router, it then forwards the TEST response back to the workstation. A REACH_ACK, which is another SSP verb, is sent between the two routers in order to establish a unique connection for these two devices within the routers. Note that both the remote workstation and front-end processor believe they are establishing a session between themselves across an SRB network that is one SRB hop away. Neither the front-end processor nor the remote workstation's software and configuration have changed.

DLSw DLC Termination and Endstation Session Initiation

After the REACH_ACK is sent, a request from the remote workstation for XID is sent to the mainframe. The XID is part of the SNA session establishment flow. Remember we saw this flow earlier in our coverage of SNA sessions. The XID is transmitted across the backbone encapsulated in TCP/IP. This allows a normal XID flow between the requesting device and the mainframe, where the workstation is uniquely identified within the SNA mainframe.

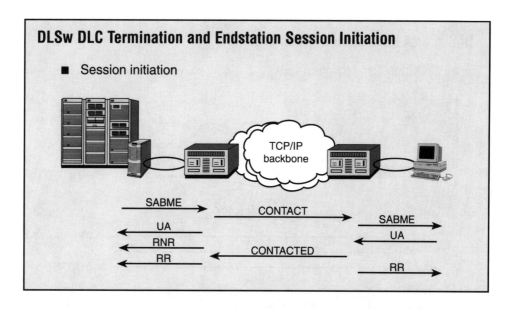

DLSw DLC Termination and Endstation Session Initiation

■ Session initiation

DLSw: SNA Endstation Session Initiation

After the XID is processed, an SABME is sent from the mainframe to the endstation. The SABME, or Set Asynchronous Balance Mode Extended, initiates the LLC2 Send and Receive counts. When the router receives the SABME, it does two things: It issues an SSP CONTACT command to the remote router and it also responds to the mainframe with an unnumbered acknowledgment (UA), initializing the LLC2 Send and Receive counts. When the remote router receives the CONTACT command, it issues an SABME to the requesting SNA workstation, initializing the Send and Receive counts. The local workstation responds back with a UA signifying that it has initialized the LLC2 Send and Receive counts. It is now ready to receive data. That signals the remote router to send an SSP CONTACTED command to the central site router.

Note that Receiver Readies (RRs) flow to the host and to the workstation independent of one another, and both are initiated and terminated by the central site and remote router. You may have noticed in this diagram that a Receiver Not Ready (RNR) was issued from the central site router between the UA and the CONTACTED frame. After the central site router sent a UA, it had to continue to tell the host that the workstation was not ready to receive information until it received verification via the CONTACTED command. This informed the central site router that the

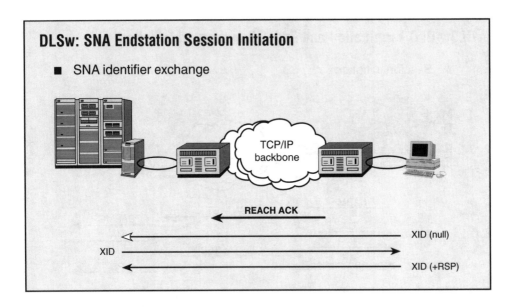

DLSw: SNA Endstation Session Initiation

■ SNA identifier exchange

TCP/IP backbone

REACH ACK

XID (null)

XID

XID (+RSP)

remote device was initialized and ready to receive data. This illustrates DLSw's ability to interpret and terminate LLC2 sessions and provide the proper flow control mechanisms between these devices.

91

DLSw: Data Transmission and Local Termination

The only traffic that passes across the enterprise backbone is SNA information frames. All the LLC2 RR frames are locally acknowledged. This ensures that both the remote workstation and the central site mainframe will not time-out and terminate sessions because of missed LLC2 RRs. DLSw also eliminates the LLC2 RR across the backbone. Remember, these are over 23 bytes long, considering a Token Ring MAC frame with a RIF field. This overhead is often omitted when calculating DLSw and comparing it to other technologies.

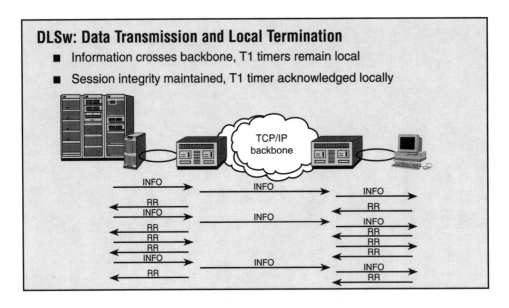

DLSw: Data Transmission and Local Termination
- Information crosses backbone, T1 timers remain local
- Session integrity maintained, T1 timer acknowledged locally

DLSw: End-to-End Flow Control

92

The slide shows that the flow control information between the mainframe and the workstation is preserved. In the example that you see here, information flows from the central site mainframe to the router, crosses the backbone, is received by the remote router, and is forwarded to the endstation. The endstation issues an LLC2 Receiver Not Ready (RNR). The RNR is received by the remote router and converted to an SSP RNR. It is then forwarded to the central site router, which then issues an RNR to the host. The RNR flows on the local LANs will continue until the remote workstation is capable of receiving information again. At that time, an LLC2 RR is sent by the remote workstation, received by the remote router, which issues an SSP RR to the central site router, which then issues the LLC2 RR to the host. This signifies to the host that the remote device is now ready to receive information.

There are several points to note: The SSP RR is designed to stop the flow of information to a specific workstation. Additional remote devices that may have started a session with the SNA mainframe are not affected. All other traffic is processed as normal. The RNRs are locally terminated on both sides of the network until an RR is sent by the remote workstation.

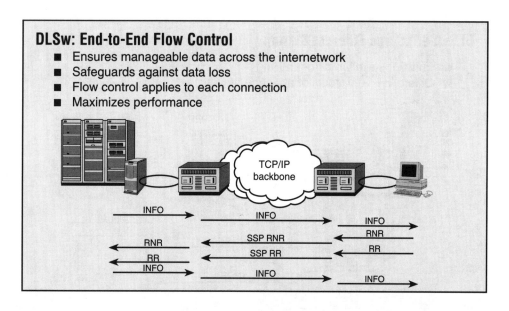

DLSw: End-to-End Flow Control
- Ensures manageable data across the internetwork
- Safeguards against data loss
- Flow control applies to each connection
- Maximizes performance

93 DLSw: SDLC and Ethernet Startup

SDLC and Ethernet session establishment is similar to the Token Ring example we just discussed. Ethernet uses LLC2 control for SNA sessions, so it is almost identical to Token Ring session establishment. One difference is that Ethernet does not use SRB; rather, a learning bridge environment is assumed by Ethernet workstations. However, the LLC2 flows and issues remain identical to the Token Ring workstation.

SDLC presents some unique problems. The slide shows an SDLC device connected to a router. The central site router is connected to the mainframe using a Token Ring gateway. The example illustrates the conversion between the SDLC and Token Ring layer 2 protocols. In this example, Set Normal Response Mode (SNRM) is sent by the remote router to the SDLC device. The SNRM will initialize the SDLC Send and Receive counts. The remote controller responds with a UA to acknowledge the SNRM and initialize the Send and Receive counts. When the remote router receives the UA, it then initiates the CANUREACH, ICANREACH, and XID sequence. However, since the SLDC does not use XID, the remote router represents the SDLC device as an LLC2 LAN-attached unit. The router needs to have a destination and source MAC address and an XID BLOCK and NUM configured to represent each SDLC-attached device. This information is mapped to a poll address for each SDLC-attached

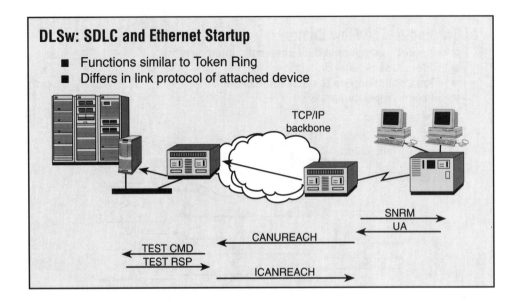

DLSw: SDLC and Ethernet Startup

- Functions similar to Token Ring
- Differs in link protocol of attached device

TCP/IP backbone

SNRM
UA
CANUREACH
TEST CMD
TEST RSP
ICANREACH

device. This function provides the link-level protocol conversion between SDLC and LLC2 traffic. The router presents the SDLC-attached device as if it is on a Token Ring LAN.

The example illustrates one a router implementation that attempts to contact the controller before contacting the host. Other implementations have the router contacting the host and establishing a session before the controller is sent the SNRM by the router. Typically, other SDLC commands can be configured to contact the SDLC-attached device.

94 DLSw: Frame Format

LSw uses a frame format based on TCP/IP and a connection protocol: Switch-to-Switch Protocol (SSP). When DLSw receives a native SNA frame, it envelops the frame with an SSP header. It then adds the TCP/IP envelope. IP ensures that this packet can be routed around failed links or routers. The TCP header guarantees that the SNA datagram will arrive at the destination host reliably and in the proper sequence.

Now let's look at an example. The DLSw interface receives an SNA frame on the Token Ring interface. The frame is sent by an SNA controller or device emulating either a PU2 or PU2.1. The first frame function DLSw performs is to remove the Token Ring MAC

frame. DLSw then takes the native SNA datagram, which consists of the SNA, TH, RH, and RU, and inserts it into an SSP frame. This frame format is then wrapped up in a TCP header. The process continues by having DLSw build an IP frame (TCP, SSP, and SNA). The IP destination address becomes the remote peer's router address. DLSw inserts its own peer address as the source. Since this is a routable IP datagram, the process is sent to the internal link processor of the router, where a proper layer 2 frame is used to send the packet along the next-hop router. Finally, the packet is queued and sent out the router interface. Each subsequent router processes the IP datagram as any other, looking up the destination IP address and forwarding the packets along. It

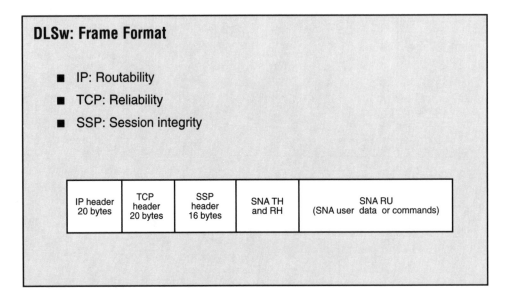

DLSw: Frame Format

- IP: Routability
- TCP: Reliability
- SSP: Session integrity

IP header 20 bytes	TCP header 20 bytes	SSP header 16 bytes	SNA TH and RH	SNA RU (SNA user data or commands)

should now be clear that DLSw needs to be configured only at the entry and exit points of the network; all intermediate routers only need IP configurations.

The description results in assembling a frame that is 56 bytes long. Each header adds some information and therefore some overhead. The SSP frame is 16 bytes long, the IP frame is 20 bytes long, and the TCP frame is also 20 bytes long. In order to optimize this frame format, multiple SNA frames could be enveloped in the same TCP/IP datagram. In order to accomplish this, the router will assemble multiple SNA frames in one TCP/IP frame. Each SNA frame is enveloped in an SSP header that uniquely identifies it to the peer router. These packets are then enveloped in TCP/IP, reducing the overhead to support these frames across the network.

95 DLSw: Overhead

Since DLSw envelops the SNA datagram in TCP/IP, it increases the overhead of the SNA packet. This can be of concern to some network analysts and designers; however, I do not believe this is a problem in the vast majority of networks. Consider the fact that IP is rapidly becoming the preferred protocol of enterprise backbones. If TCP/IP produces undesirable overhead, why would you consider migrating your data applications to TCP/IP by building mission-critical applications using TCP/IP? Why have an enterprise TCP/IP network?

In a TCP/IP application environment, every transaction has the overhead associated with TCP/IP. In addition, several integration techniques, such as TN3270(E), use TCP/IP to transport 3270 SNA information. As you will see later, TN3270 may be the simplest and most cost-effective way to integrate SNA into your intranet. TN3270 transactions generate about the same overhead as DLSw for each 3270 transaction. My one major caution in selecting an SNA integration technology is to clearly understand the overhead of a technology. This can be difficult and deceiving in some cases. I am often asked about frame relay's ability to transport SNA traffic, and it is believed to be preferred because of a reduction in overhead. I do not argue against frame relay being a good integration technology; however, as we will see in the next several sections, frame relay uses LLC2 and, in some implemen-

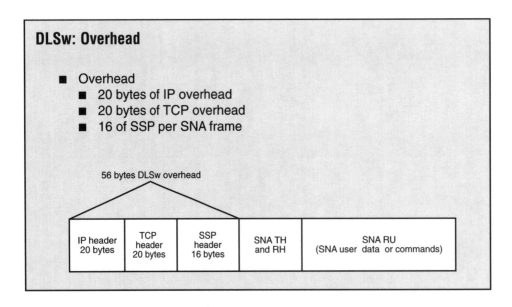

tations, a Token Ring MAC header. Although the LLC2 and Token Ring MAC produce less overhead than a DLSw frame, the fact that LLC2 requires both acknowledgment RR frames and the continual RR "keep-alive" polls is not considered in the overhead. Be careful and consider the entire overhead generated by a particular solution and protocol.

96

DLSw: Compression

A benefit of DLSw in a router environment is the use of router data compression. Many of today's routers offer this as either a hardware or software option. This is a very powerful tool that will improve performance of the network.

Compression dramatically increases (typically, doubles) the available bandwidth between two locations. This allows the network designer to build networks that support more users, while increasing the performance and reducing the reoccurring telecommunications costs. Specifically, greater bandwidth helps ensure predictable performance and reduces the response time of SNA transactions.

When DLSw is implemented in routers, many of the advanced features that router vendors offer can also be used. Router compression is one such feature. It reduces the overhead associated with DLSw and reduces the size of SNA and other protocols' packets. This greatly improves the amount of bandwidth available to all of your remote applications. I strongly recommend running compression on your router to support SNA applications.

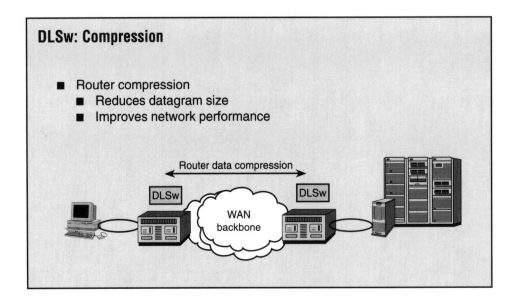

DLSw: Compression

- Router compression
  - Reduces datagram size
  - Improves network performance

Router data compression

DLSw

WAN backbone

DLSw

There is a difference between enveloping and encapsulation. Consider this definition: Encapsulation is a method that wraps a layer 2 frame around the received layer 2 frame from the router's interface. It is used by the oldest methods to transport SNA traffic through your network. This includes IP encapsulation of LAN frames and SDLC encapsulation of SDLC link-level frames.

For an example of an encapsulation data frame, consider a Token Ring frame that is received on a router interface and encapsulated in IP/UDP. The router receives an SNA Token Ring frame. This frame is comprised of the 802.5 Token Ring MAC header, an LLC2 header, and the native SNA frame (TH/RH/RU). Encapsulation is then performed by adding an UDP datagram, which provides layer 4 application support. A layer 3 IP header is added to provide the network address and to complete datagram encapsulation. The frame is then sent to the outbound link interface where a layer 2 header is added, and the packet is then sent to the next-hop router. As you can see, encapsulation generates quite a bit of additional frame overhead. Since the entire received frame is encapsulated, it does not provide conversion between link-layer protocols. Whatever is received on the inbound interface (in this case, Token Ring) must be sent on the same type of interface on the remote side. Additionally, this implementation does not provide local termination.

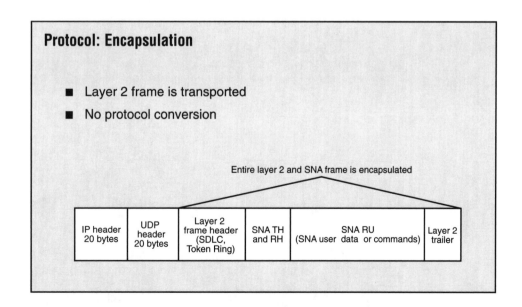

Protocol: Encapsulation

- Layer 2 frame is transported
- No protocol conversion

Entire layer 2 and SNA frame is encapsulated

| IP header 20 bytes | UDP header 20 bytes | Layer 2 frame header (SDLC, Token Ring) | SNA TH and RH | SNA RU (SNA user data or commands) | Layer 2 trailer |

Every LLC2 frame that is sent between the source and destination (for example, a source device such as a 3174 controller and a destination device such as a mainframe) must cross the network and be encapsulated by the method just described.

To summarize, encapsulation generates quite a bit of additional overhead. Overhead is generated by adding a completely new protocol frame to the received datagram and by encapsulating all layer 2 flow controls and acknowledgments (LLC2 information on LAN interfaces and SDLC polls when processing SDLC link interfaces). Encapsulation does not provide support for link-level protocol conversion. This forces the sending and receiving stations to be on the same media type (Token Ring to Token Ring, SDLC to SDLC). In order to correct these deficiencies, let's look at my definition of *enveloping*.

Enveloping solves the problems generated by encapsulation. It reduces the overhead associated with encapsulation by eliminating the incoming layer 2 frame. Also, since the frame is "terminated," it must also respond to the link-layer acknowledgments (LLC2 control flows and SDLC polls). Additionally, because it does not transport the incoming layer 2 frame, it can convert between layer 2 protocols. For example, SNA traffic received from an SDLC or Ethernet interface is sent to the destination devices on a Token Ring interface.

Now let's look at an example of a enveloped frame. An SNA datagram is received on an Ethernet interface. The layer 2 MAC header is dropped. Since the layer 2 information also contains LLC2 information, the interface processes the LLC2 request and sends a response back to the sending workstation. Enveloping processes the remaining SNA frame (the SNA, TH, RH, and RU) and assembles a new frame by adding an IP header for layer 3 routing and, typically, a TCP header for reliable transmission. (Remember, we just provided the link acknowledgment to the sending stations. We need to guarantee delivery across the network.) The frame is then sent to the link interface where a layer 2 header is added and sent to the next-hop router.

This is the same technique that any IP packet flow experiences in the network; in fact, it happens all the time within your cur-

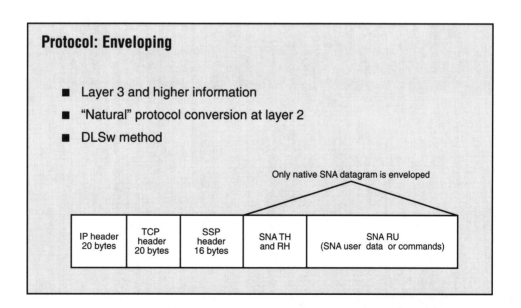

Protocol: Enveloping

- Layer 3 and higher information
- "Natural" protocol conversion at layer 2
- DLSw method

Only native SNA datagram is enveloped

| IP header 20 bytes | TCP header 20 bytes | SSP header 16 bytes | SNA TH and RH | SNA RU (SNA user data or commands) |

rent network. Imagine a TCP/IP workstation on an Ethernet wanting to connect to a TCP/IP server on an FDDI backbone. The datagram is received on the router's Ethernet interface. The router removes the Ethernet MAC layer or link layer and examines the TCP/IP datagram. It determines that this datagram must be forwarded out to an FDDI ring. It then builds an FDDI MAC layer header and envelops the TCP/IP datagram. So, to process TCP/IP traffic through the router, all we do is change the IP datagrams of the envelope. This is similar to DLSw.

DLSw uses enveloping. In addition to the frame assembly just described, DLSw adds an SSP (Switch-to-Switch Protocol) header to the SNA frame before the IP header. SSP uniquely identifies each SNA PU and provides the proper flow control mechanisms and session controls (startup and termination).

This technique provides DLSw with reroutability (IP), reliability (TCP), and native layer 2 protocol conversion—a very important and valuable feature for SNA networks. This provides the capability to have remote attached SDLC, Ethernet, and, of course, Token Ring devices and have them connect to a channel-attached Token Ring gateway such as a 3745 FEP.

DLSw: Scalability Enhancements

> **DLSw: Scalability Enhancements**
> - Router processor speed
> - Over 800 MB of memory
> - TCP sessions

DLSw routers need to scale to support large enterprise SNA networks. Scaling DLSw must include support for a large number of remote locations and many SNA PUs. DLSw ability to scale is a result of several factors. DLSw networks started being deployed over four years ago. This has allowed the code to mature, and the industry has gained experience in building large DLSw networks.

DLSw can be resource intensive because many TCP connections are needed in large networks, along with SNA physical units. The amount of memory and the capacity of the CPU in routers have greatly increased the ability of these networks to scale. As mentioned earlier, older router technology was based on 286 and 386 classes of CPUs. Today's routers are based on high-speed RISC or Pentium II-type processors. Also, the available memory in routers has greatly increased. The largest routers have over 800 megabytes of memory.

100 DLSw: Vendor-Specific Enhancements

DLSw is documented in three RFCs, which we will discuss in the next several sections. Like most standards, vendors often develop enhancements, some of which prohibit interoperability. Others provide enhancements that result in "better than" standard implementations. Before we look at the RFCs, let's look at some vendor enhancements to DLSw.

Router vendors have added several enhancements that allow you to grow and maintain a large DLSw network. One of the most important is the ability to provide support for unconfigured DLSw peer routers. This feature allows a router to configure its peers, and have the peers accept incoming requests

to establish a DLSw session. Remember, when DLSw initiates a session, it directs the SSP CANUREACH discovery frames to specific routers. Tables are normally configured in each router to identify the potential peer routers. Since legacy SNA is a host-centric system, all traffic is typically directed to the SNA mainframe located in the corporate data center. This results in simpler network designs and configuration of DLSw routers, since all the remote routers peer to a central data center router. The unconfigured peers enhancement provides the ability to configure the peer on one side of the connection. Defining the peer router address reduces the peer address management and cuts the configuration of peers in half.

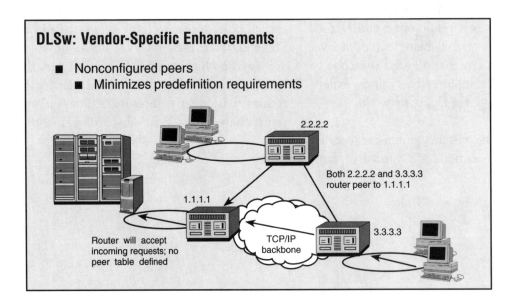

DLSw: Vendor-Specific Enhancements
- Nonconfigured peers
  - Minimizes predefinition requirements

2.2.2.2

Both 2.2.2.2 and 3.3.3.3 router peer to 1.1.1.1

1.1.1.1

TCP/IP backbone

3.3.3.3

Router will accept incoming requests; no peer table defined

DLSw: Bandwidth Management

101

DLSw: Bandwidth Management

- Ensures multiprotocol network can meet service-level agreements for SNA users

- Priority forwarding and guaranteed bandwidth for specified traffic
    - Multiple queues
    - Service level defined for each queue

- Predefined or user-defined criteria
    - User 1 preference over user 2
    - Interactive displays preference over printers
    - SNA preference over netbios

DLSw does not provide a native prioritization scheme; however, many routers provide this capability in a number of fashions. The most basic is the ability of a router to prioritize TCP/IP traffic on the WAN interface. The simplest way to accomplish this for DLSw is to define a router priority filter to place TCP ports 2065 and 2067 in the high-priority queue. These ports are the common transmit and receive DLSw TCP ports defined in the original DLSw RFC, 1434. Newer RFCs allow the ability to use a single TCP port for DLSw and also identify the DLSw port number. If your implementation provides this feature, use your defined port number and develop a filter to put this in the high-priority queue. This simple filter ensures that all SNA traffic exiting the router's WAN interface will receive priority over all other traffic.

In addition to basic router priority cues, many vendors have implemented DLSw priority cues. These priority queues manage bandwidth for various SNA traffic. For example, SNA traffic destined to a 3745 MAC address may have a higher priority than file transfer traffic using the MAC address of a FTP server. Filtering on a bit in the FID2 TH or RH may provide certain responses to get a higher-priority queue. For example, to specify a higher priority for terminal traffic, you can build a filter to put print traffic in a low-priority queue. This can be determined if your site has a set of standards and printers are always configured using a common local address. The FID2 header Local Address field can be filtered to identify printers and assign the printer traffic to a low-priority queue. DLSw priority filters are implemented on the local router, so there are no vendor interoperability issues.

There is no DLSw priority scheme defined in the RFCs. Providing SNA a high priority is a very popular topic. Vendors like to talk about it because it allows them to distinguish features above and beyond what is normally defined in the DLSw RFCs. However, my experience shows that priority is typically overrated by customers and not used in many networks. Most users want to hear about various priority schemes; however, they do not implement them. There is a simple reason for this: SNA traffic was designed to work in a pre-AT&T divested world. This world was comprised of low-speed lines (4.6 links, 9.6 links), and in order to save money, these remote locations shared bandwidth by implementing multidrop SDLC circuits. Consider that devices are still running the same legacy SNA applications, but have been converted to a router network that is based on line speeds of at least 56 kilobits per second. This gives the remote location and the 3270 application more bandwidth than ever imagined. As legacy devices are converted to high-speed 10- or 16-megabit LAN interfaces or to higher-speed SDLC point-to-point lines connected to the back of the router, their performance increases as the response time improves.

Another SDLC feature provides primary link station support. This feature allows a router to be polled by a front-end processor. Most SDLC devices are supported in secondary mode. Secondary mode supports SDLC-attached control units, or PU2.0 and PU2.1 devices.

SDLC's primary support, the router, is actually attached typically to a front-end processor, such as a 3745, and is polled by that 3745. The fact that the router has to respond to the SDLC polls presents some challenges in router codes. However, this feature is supported by most vendors who implement DLSw. I would only recommend this technology for sites that have very old mainframes and have no LAN attachment devices supporting SNA traffic in that environment. In fact, if the customer or you are committed to long-term SNA connectivity and have this environment, I would strongly encourage you to provide connectivity through any one of the various gateways that we discussed earlier and use a LAN access to the mainframe. LAN access is much easier to configure and a much better performer than the secondary SDLC.

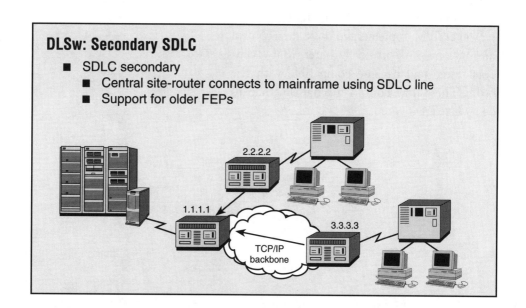

DLSw: Secondary SDLC
- SDLC secondary
  - Central site-router connects to mainframe using SDLC line
  - Support for older FEPs

DLSw: Original RFC 1434

DLSw: Original RFC 1434

- What does RFC 1434 provide?
    - RFC 1434 defines basic data flows
        - Switch-to-switch protocol
    - Rate-based flow control
        - Already provided in Bay Networks' routers

- What does RFC 1434 not provide?
    - Does not address scalability
        - This is the only planned enhancement for version 2
    - Flow control features
        - Reverse engineering

RFC 1434 was the original DLSw RFC. It defined basic data flows for the SSP protocol. Many rate-based protocols that define flow control were not specified in the RFC. However, IBM implemented these flow control mechanisms with its 6611 router. Many vendors tested and became compatible with the 6611. These flow control mechanisms had to be reverse engineered.

DLSw: Version 1: RFC 1795

104

DLSw: Version 1: RFC 1795

- What does RFC 1795 provide?
  - RFC 1795 defines more data flows
  - Capabilities exchange
    - Interoperability
  - Rate-based flow control
- What does RFC 1795 not provide?
  - Does not address scalability
    - This is the only planned enhancement for version 2

What does RFC 1795 provide? Basically it defines all of the reverse engineering flows that were accomplished by the vendors in the previous RFC. Since RFC 1434 was negligent in that area and everyone reengineered them, they were documented in RFC 1795. In addition to that, a rate-based flow control mechanism was specifically defined, along with the capabilities exchange to provide easier interoperability between vendors. Still, RFC 1795 did not address scalability, and that will happen in the next RFC. There is very little difference between RFC 1434 and RFC 1795. In fact, for most customers, I would recommend they stay on RFC 1434 and not migrate to RFC

1795 because there is virtually no distinction in performance and enhancement capabilities between those RFCs. RFC 1795 superseded 1434 because it clarified many of the points that RFC 1434 did not discuss, such as flow control mechanisms and capabilities exchange. It is also known as DLSw Version 1. If I was to implement the new DLSw version, I would probably take the vendor default. There is very little difference in these two RFCs. By taking the vendor default, you are typically getting the method the vendor feels most comfortable implementing. The only time I would recommend RFC1795 is when you need to interoperate between multiple router vendors.

105

DLSw: Version 2: RFC 2166

> ## DLSw: Version 2: RFC 2166
>
> - What does RFC 2166 provide?
>   - Scalability enhancements
>   - UDP explorers
>   - Reduces TCP connections
>   - Multicast support
>   - Ease of configuration
>   - TCP connection time-outs

RFC 2166 provides scalability enhancements and this is done in a variety of ways. The first and most dramatic is that UDP datagrams are used for the SSP CANUREACH/ICANREACH explorers. Note that in the example previously discussed, a TCP connection was established between the two routers *before* the SSP explorers were sent. TCP connections increase the overhead in routers. For the remote router that is communicating to a central site, it is probably very trivial. However, at the central site, this could be a very large burden, especially in large networks where you have lots of remote routers and, therefore, TCP connections. These connections need be established before the ICANREACH or CANUREACH explorer frames are exchanged.

Version 2 of DLSw provides the capability of using a UDP datagram for the SNA explorer, negating the necessity to establish any TCP sessions for explorer exchange. This is most helpful when the enterprise supports multiple host or server locations or multiple central site routers for redundancy and load balancing. However, many SNA enterprises have a single mainframe and require connections for the majority of a business day. In this environment, the UDP datagram will not save any significant overhead because a TCP connection is required all the time. But, even in these environments, if multiple routers are used for backup and redundancy, fewer TCP sessions should be required. A TCP session with the primary router would be required, but only TCP sessions with backup routers are necessary when the primary fails or becomes too congested. RFC 2166 reduces the number of TCP sessions in the network.

Another capability of RFC 2166 is that it will time-out TCP sessions that have not transmitted any user information in a defined time interval. This will reduce unneeded TCP sessions and only reestablish them when the user decides to access the SNA host. Again, the number of TCP connections is reduced at the central site.

Another feature of DLSw v2 is multicast support. Multicast provides easier configuration and control of the SNA network. A single multicast address can be configured to respond to DLSw's explorer requests and DLSw router capabilities. A router only needs to listen to the single IP multicast address. Configuration of the routers is easier, since a single IP address can be used throughout the enterprise in order support all SNA devices and DLSw partner routers.

DLSw provides the seamless integration of SNA traffic across a company's intranet. We already discussed various protocols and technology used by DLSw to reliably transport SNA traffic. It uses TCP, which guarantees that SNA traffic is delivered reliably and in the proper order. IP is used to provide the ability to reroute traffic around failed network resources. A third protocol is defined by the RFCs that establishes, terminates, and provides flow control to various SNA sessions. Link-level protocol support includes Ethernet, Token Ring, FDDI, frame relay, and SDLC.

DLSw can best be described as a TCP/IP application. It will only perform as well as your IP network and can only exist on an IP network. One of the biggest mistakes you can make is trying to debug a DLSw network while not knowing if your IP network is functioning properly. Always make sure the TCP/IP network is operating before attempting to install DLSw between routers.

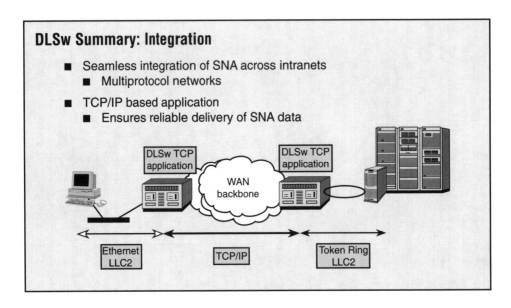

DLSw Summary: Integration

- ■ Seamless integration of SNA across intranets
  - ■ Multiprotocol networks
- ■ TCP/IP based application
  - ■ Ensures reliable delivery of SNA data

One of the fundamental proposes of DLSw is to protect your investment in SNA hardware and software. It accomplishes this by supporting your SNA hardware and the various SNA link interfaces. You keep your SDLC-attached controller, your SDLC workstation, and your Token Ring-attached workstation without changing any of the software or hardware interfaces on these devices. You do not even have to change the configuration of any of these devices. In addition, and more importantly, it protects your investment in the 3270 applications that reside on your mainframe. These applications have been running your business, and you may realize that you cannot cost justify moving those 3270 applications off to other servers. In fact, more and more enterprises are realizing the mainframe performs

extremely well as a traditional SNA host along with a IP application server.

DLSw also supports a variety of different layer 2 interfaces (link interfaces) such as Token Ring, Ethernet, and SDLC. Token Ring and SDLC are the most popular SNA link-level protocols; however, many customers are also converting or installing new SNA devices using Ethernet. SNA Ethernet networks are rapidly becoming a viable and popular option in most remote locations. DLSw allows the seamless mixing of link-level interfaces. It provides native link-level protocol conversion between any support interfaces. Typically, remote locations will have Ethernet and SDLC devices that attach to the mainframe using a traditional Token Ring gateway.

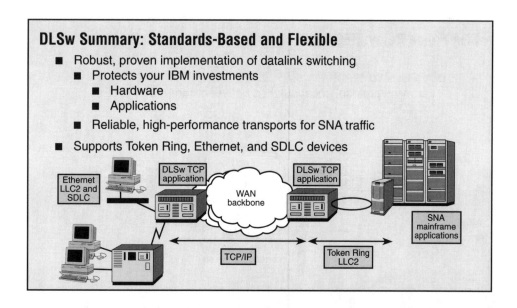

DLSw Summary: Standards-Based and Flexible
- Robust, proven implementation of datalink switching
  - Protects your IBM investments
    - Hardware
    - Applications
  - Reliable, high-performance transports for SNA traffic
- Supports Token Ring, Ethernet, and SDLC devices

108 SNA Frame Relay: RFC 1490

RFC 1490 is typically referred to as an SNA integration technique. RFC 1490 can support SNA devices, but has no direct relationship to SNA, nor was it specially developed for SNA devices. The RFC defines how data is encapsulated between two frame relay devices. It allows multiple protocols to share the same frame relay connection (DLCI) as the SNA traffic. SNA datagrams are encapsulated using RFC 1490 and appear like native SNA traffic in a bridged format. That is, it envelops the SNA traffic in an LLC2 header (and has all the issues that LLC2 presents) and adds an RFC 1490 header. This method is called *Boundary Network Node* (BNN). Another method envelops the SNA datagram in LLC2 and a Token Ring MAC header. This is called *Boundary Access Node* (BAN).

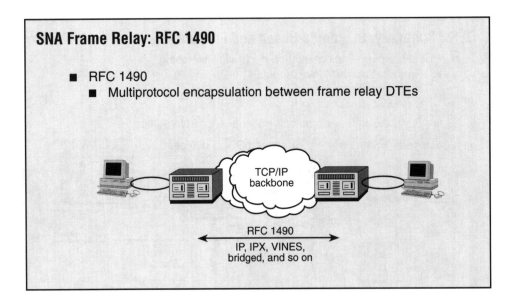

SNA Frame Relay: RFC 1490

- RFC 1490
  - Multiprotocol encapsulation between frame relay DTEs

TCP/IP backbone

RFC 1490
IP, IPX, VINES, bridged, and so on

RFC 1490 enveloping is really a single-switch datalinked switch. A remote Frame Relay Access Device (FRAD) removes the layer 2 Token Ring, Ethernet, or SDLC frame and envelops the native SNA datagram in an LLC2 (BNN) or LLC2 and Token Ring MAC (BAN) header. Then it envelops the new frame in a frame relay RFC 1490 header. This is exactly the function a single-switch datalink switch performs, except that in most cases, the single-switch datalink switch converts SDLC to a Token Ring frame.

RFC 1490 defines the enveloping method for layer 2 and 3 protocols across a frame relay network: "Routed" SNA or BNN in routed layer 3 enveloping. BNN inserts the native SNA datagram (TH/RH/RU) in an LLC2 and then an RFC 1490 header. The packet can then be transmitted across the frame relay network. Note that LLC2 control is used to provide SNA with reliable transmissions between two frame relay DTEs. All the overhead characteristics of LLC2 we discussed earlier are present. In addition, the frame relay DTE also uniquely identifies each SNA device. A unique SNA Service Access Point (SAP) is used in the LLC2 header to uniquely identify each individual device. For example, in a network with 100 remote SNA devices, 100 SNA SAPs are required to uniquely identify all devices. This results in tables that must be configured to map each device with a different SAP address. This can be a bit time consuming and also has repercussions in recovery capabilities.

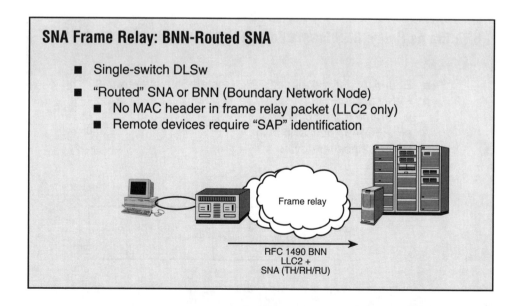

SNA Frame Relay: BNN-Routed SNA

- Single-switch DLSw

- "Routed" SNA or BNN (Boundary Network Node)
  - No MAC header in frame relay packet (LLC2 only)
  - Remote devices require "SAP" identification

Frame relay

RFC 1490 BNN
LLC2 +
SNA (TH/RH/RU)

SNA Frame Relay: BNN Frame Format

The slide illustrates the frame relay "routed" SNA or BNN frame format. The first field contains the link header information. This is equivalent to an HDLC or SDLC frame. The second field is the RFC 1490 header that identifies the type of packet. Finally, the last field describes protocol headers that are used to envelop the SNA datagram. Note that the BNN header is significantly shorter than BAN by at least 16 bytes. Note that each LLC2 RR poll and acknowledgment will also have this frame format.

SNA Frame Relay: BNN Frame Format

- Boundary network node BNN: Routed SNA over frame
- Relay packet=
  - Frame format 6 bytes +
  - RFC1490 header 6 bytes +
  - LLC2 header 4bytes +
  - Data

FLAG (1)	Link address (2)	Frame relay protocol header	LLC2 and SNA data	FCS (2)	FLAG (1)

SNA Frame Relay: Bridged SNA—BAN

Boundary Access Node (BAN) is the second enveloping technique for SNA over a frame relay network. BAN is similar to BNN except that, along with an LLC2 header, the SNA datagram is also enveloped using an 802.5 Token Ring MAC header. The MAC header provides the capability to identify each SNA device with a MAC address, eliminating the unique SAP addressing. Note that LLC2 control is still used to ensure reliable delivery of SNA information.

Using a MAC frame provides benefits over SAP multiplexing described earlier. We can uniquely identify each workstation with its native LAN MAC address. We still need to map MAC addresses to SDLC-attached devices; however, this is typically less time consuming since there are normally fewer PUs on SDLC lines than on LANs. BAN also provides better load balancing, and it is easier to use a second redundant link, especially when connecting directly to an SNA FEP.

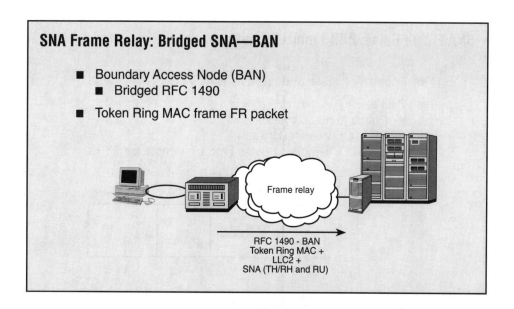

SNA Frame Relay: Bridged SNA—BAN

- Boundary Access Node (BAN)
  - Bridged RFC 1490
- Token Ring MAC frame FR packet

Frame relay

RFC 1490 - BAN
Token Ring MAC +
LLC2 +
SNA (TH/RH and RU)

112

SNA Frame Relay: BAN Frame Format

Ban uses a more traditionally bridged frame. This packet has, of course, the frame format of 6 bytes and the RFC 1490 header that includes 8 bytes of information. In addition, a MAC/LLC header is included. This is 17 bytes with up to 16 more bytes for a RIF field. As you can see, this is a variable-length field and is much closer to a DLSw frame in overhead. Also note that LLC2 RR polls and acknowledgments have the same frame format.

SNA Frame Relay: BAN Frame Format

- Boundary Access Node (BAN): Bridged SNA over frame
- Packet =
  - Frame format 6 bytes +
  - FRC1490 header 8 bytes +
  - MAC/LLC header 17 bytes (+up to 16 more for RIF) +
  - Data

FLAG (1)	Link address (2)	Frame relay protocol header	MAC,LLC2 and SNA data	FCS (2)	FLAG (1)

RFC 1490 "bridges" SNA traffic across the WAN. Frame relay advocates typically proclaim frame relay as a preferred protocol because it has a smaller frame size. This is a result of the simpler RFC 1490 header and bridged frame format. However, normally not discussed is the additional overhead that is incurred because of the LLC2 RR polls and acknowledgments. LLC2 polls and acknowledgments must be included in any overhead discussion. This traffic is often difficult to identify, since the amount of overhead is determined by your message sizes and arrival rates.

So, what is the right answer? Ignore it! If the amount of overhead that a DLSw TCP/IP frame generates may be a concern to you, ask yourself why you are implementing TCP/IP applications. Why are you increasing the "overhead" on that simple SDLC multidrop line? Why would you ever want to leave the world of efficient 3270 SNA applications? If we all thought in these terms, we would have never implemented PCs and would still be communicating with TTY and bisynchronous protocols. To determine the overhead in your environment is far too time consuming, and I expect that the differences will be far too trivial to be of much concern.

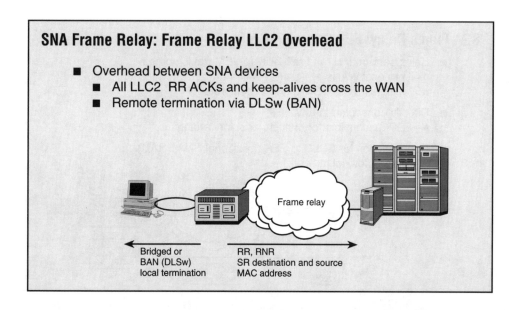

SNA Frame Relay: Frame Relay LLC2 Overhead

- Overhead between SNA devices
  - All LLC2 RR ACKs and keep-alives cross the WAN
  - Remote termination via DLSw (BAN)

Bridged or
BAN (DLSw)
local termination

Frame relay

RR, RNR
SR destination and source
MAC address

114

SNA Frame Relay: FEP Connection

rame relay helps the performance and relia- bility of SNA traffic across the WAN. This is accomplished by using multiple PVCs for per- formance and LLC2 for reliability. For example, a remote device could use a single PVC to transport SNA traffic and another PVC to trans- port non-SNA data. By having different PVCs and traffic shaping, you could control the amount of bandwidth designated for SNA. This is typically locally configured on the remote device and would be similar to various router pri- ority schemes that we discussed earlier.

Frame relay is also supported by the FEP, allowing you to directly connect the remote FRADs to the SNA host. The FEP does a great job with SNA; however, it does a very poor job with other protocols. In fact, it pro- vides no protocol support for some of the devices. However, in single-protocol environ- ment (SNA) that can cost justify a frame relay network over the existing multidrop SNA network, this becomes a very cost-effective solution to transport SNA traffic. Of course, this assumes that you are not going to inte- grate other protocols into your enterprise, which is a very big assumption, and probably one that is not very realistic in most environ- ments. Nevertheless, this can be an excellent solution for the enterprise that wants to con- vert SDLC devices to frame relay and leverage FEP into the frame relay backbone.

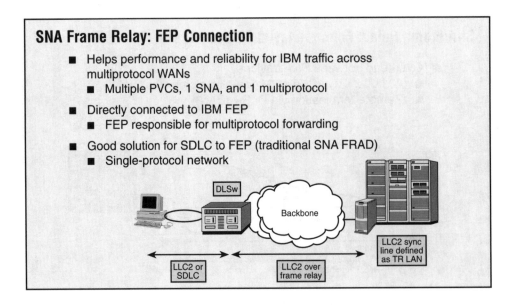

SNA Frame Relay: FEP Connection

- Helps performance and reliability for IBM traffic across multiprotocol WANs
  - Multiple PVCs, 1 SNA, and 1 multiprotocol
- Directly connected to IBM FEP
  - FEP responsible for multiprotocol forwarding
- Good solution for SDLC to FEP (traditional SNA FRAD)
  - Single-protocol network

DLSw

Backbone

LLC2 sync line defined as TR LAN

LLC2 or SDLC

LLC2 over frame relay

Another alternative to connecting to frame relay and using either BAN or BNN is to connect to a central site router instead of the FEP. This configuration still provides the capability of supporting multiple PVCs, dedicating one for SNA and one for other multiprotocol traffic. By directly connecting to a router, you remove the FEP from directly attaching to the frame relay network, thereby lowering its price and leveraging the higher-performance LAN interfaces such as Token Ring. This solution also provides better multiprotocol integration because the router can natively route IP/IPX, AppleTalk, and so forth, instead of the very limited support provided by the FEP.

There is a lingering issue when using BAN or BNN to support SNA traffic across the frame relay network. Both BAN and BNN integration uses LLC2 to provide reliable transmission of SNA traffic. LLC2 generates additional overhead due to RR polls and acknowledgments. If the frame relay network becomes congested, and LLC2 packets are either discarded or not delivered, SNA sessions may time-out because of a low tolerance of missed information. Remember that LLC2 was designed for, and works best in, a LAN environment. The additional overhead and issues surrounding LLC2 to deliver SNA traffic are often understated when RFC 1490 is discussed.

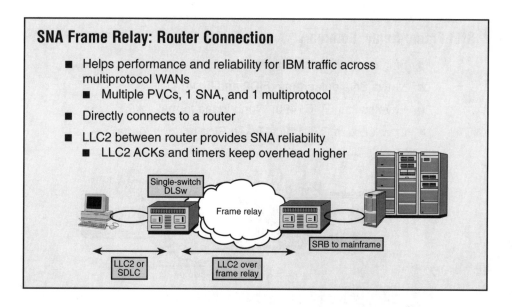

SNA Frame Relay: Router Connection

- Helps performance and reliability for IBM traffic across multiprotocol WANs
    - Multiple PVCs, 1 SNA, and 1 multiprotocol
- Directly connects to a router
- LLC2 between router provides SNA reliability
    - LLC2 ACKs and timers keep overhead higher

Single-switch DLSw

Frame relay

SRB to mainframe

LLC2 or SDLC

LLC2 over frame relay

116

SNA Frame Relay: Summary

Frame relay really defines a single-switch, datalink switching environment. As the router or FRAD receives an SNA packet, it removes the layer 2 frame. It envelops native SNA datagrams in LLC2 and an RFC 1490 header and transmits them across a frame relay network. It also provides local acknowledgment to the sending SNA device. This is the identical operation of a single-switch DLSw router. LLC2 control is used as a flow control mechanism between the two frame relay DTEs.

The FEP's support of RFC 1490 and frame relay does provide unique design considerations. It allows the FEP to be directly connected to the frame relay network and communicate with a remote router to support SNA devices. In a more traditional configuration, the remote router, or FRAD, is also connected to a central site router. The central site router can then convert the SNA packet to any protocol that is supported by the FEP.

One advantage of frame rely is that SNA devices can be directly connected to a FEP, and frame overhead can be minimized. The disadvantages include a bridged type network with LLC2 overhead and time-out considerations. Additionally, multiprotocol support can be more costly and, based on the design broadcast storm, can become a problem.

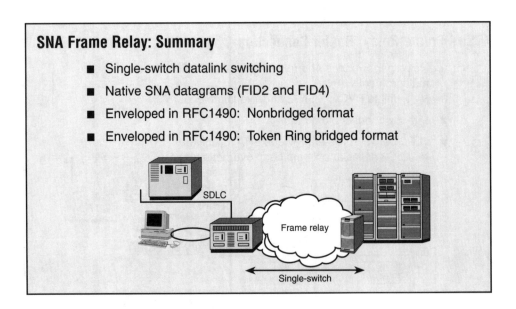

SNA Frame Relay: Summary

- Single-switch datalink switching
- Native SNA datagrams (FID2 and FID4)
- Enveloped in RFC1490: Nonbridged format
- Enveloped in RFC1490: Token Ring bridged format

SDLC

Frame relay

Single-switch

Advanced Peer-to-Peer Networking (APPN)

Now, we are going to explore APPN, or Advanced Peer-to-Peer Networking technology. APPN is a new SNA architecture that transitions traditional SNA into a distributed client/server environment. Specifically, it provides native support for logical unit LU6.2 and client/server applications based on this new LU type.

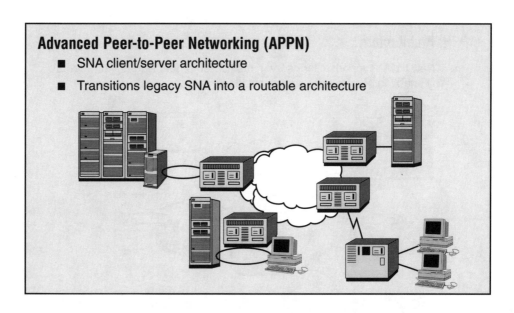

Advanced Peer-to-Peer Networking (APPN)
- SNA client/server architecture
- Transitions legacy SNA into a routable architecture

118   APPN: Architecture

The "New SNA" is designed to support client/server applications in distributed processing environments. It enables peer-to-peer communications without requiring information to be set up through an IBM mainframe. This provides a more robust network with the capabilities enjoyed by contemporary network protocols. That is, SNA routers can learn the network's topology, determine the best route within the network, and support communications between devices. This is accomplished without having to rely on a host for session setup, while still supporting the ability to enable and disable SNA sessions.

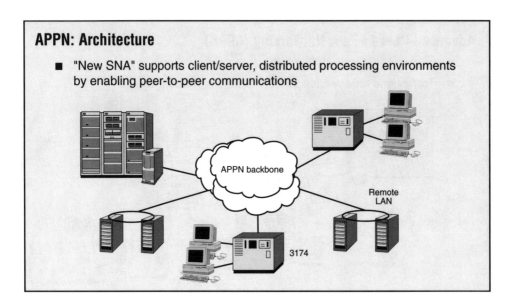

APPN: Architecture

- "New SNA" supports client/server, distributed processing environments by enabling peer-to-peer communications

APPN backbone

Remote LAN

3174

APPN: SNA Router (Network Node) 119

APPN: SNA Router (Network Node)

- As the APPN routers, NNs form the APPN backbone by
  - Exchanging topology information
  - Cooperating with other NNs in network searches
- Network nodes' provided services
  - Location of network resources (LUs)
  - Route calculation
  - Session routing

APPN architectures defines several node types: The network node (NN) is the APPN router. It provides the capability to forward datagrams within the APPN environment. Its functions include learning the network and exchanging topology information with other NNs. There are some benefits with APPN that traditional routers do not have. Each APPN NN establishes a unique session with every device that requires support for network services. This is similar to defining a default gateway in a workstation in an IP network. However, the APPN workstation, or End Node (EN), establishes a session with its "gateway" SNA router. The NN node learns the various services that this device has to offer and provides services to the EN. These include the ability to network resources, establish a session, and define session characteristics, which includes very robust Class of Service (CoS) support.

This is a very powerful function on the APPN network. It eliminates the coding of SNA definitions, which were required in the legacy SNA network.

APPN: Building Blocks

There are three basic node types for APPN: The Network Node (NN), as we briefly discussed, is the APPN router. It provides topology information and route calculation based on a variety of different parameters that we will see in a few moments.

The second component is the APPN End Node (EN). An EN is any host that requires services from the network. This can include workstations, PC terminal controllers, mini-systems and, of course, mainframes.

APPN architecture requires that ENs establish a session with a NN in order to communicate with other devices. It builds a connection-oriented session between these two devices, called a Control Point (CP) session. CP sessions are also established between NN. The CP session allows NN to exchange topology information and ENs to communicate the services or applications they have to offer and provides node-to-node communications.

Another device is called a LEN, or Low Entry Networking. It is actually a pre-EN host and does not have the capability of bringing up a CP session. It is a device that requires static definitions in order to use the APPN network services and applications. In order to support LEN devices, the NNs need statically defined information about the LEN.

These three node types, NN, EN, and LENs, along with the CP session form the backbone of the APPN network.

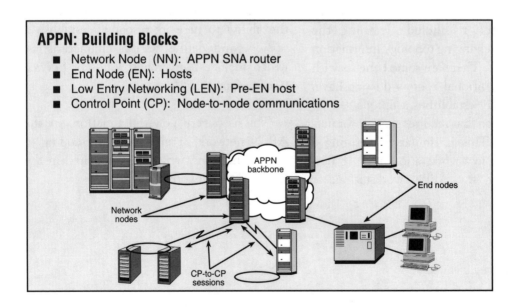

APPN: Building Blocks
- Network Node (NN): APPN SNA router
- End Node (EN): Hosts
- Low Entry Networking (LEN): Pre-EN host
- Control Point (CP): Node-to-node communications

APPN backbone

End nodes

Network nodes

CP-to-CP sessions

APPN: Intermediate Session Routing (ISR) 121

There are two fundamental protocols defined in the APPN stack: The original protocol suite is known as Intermediate Session Routing (ISR). ISR had several major drawbacks that delayed its acceptance. These included no dynamic routing and very slow node processing. A newer protocol was introduced to resolve these issues. It is called HPR, or High-Performance Routing.

APPN was first deployed supporting only ISR routing capabilities. ISR uses a label-swapping technique to forward datagrams across the network. A Local Session Format Identifier (LSFID) is used to identify the going port of the local router. The APPN router changes the address of the SNA packets, "tagging" it with an identifier of the next router interface. This ID has only local significance in the Network Node.

ISR issues a connection-oriented protocol at each hop. It is the responsibility of each router to ensure that the packets are received error free and in sequence. This inhibits ISR's capability to recover on a node failure. Because each node has end-to-end session integrity and guaranteed delivery, if a particular link or node fails, the session has to restart. Also, because we are doing session recovery in each of the nodes, there is a lot of overhead in doing hop-by-hop error checking and packet sequencing.

ISR was the first APPN implementation. It had several problems, which we described. Most users who want to implement APPN should look at deploying the newer APPN protocols defined in HPR.

122
APPN: High-Performance Routing (HPR)

APPN: High-Performance Routing (HPR)

- APPN: HPR
  - A reliable transport service
    - Rapid Transport Protocol (RTP)
  - High-performance network service (connectionless)
    - Automatic Network Routing (ANR)

High-Performance Routing (HPR) is a peer-to-peer APPN SNA network protocol suite that is similar in function and architecture to TCP/IP. Unlike ISR, HPR does provide dynamic routing. It is based on two protocols: Rapid Transport Protocol (RTP), which is similar to TCP, and ANR, which is connectionless and similar to IP. RTP guarantees reliable transmission of information between two endstations. Like TCP, it is based on an OSI Class 4 transport, which has these capabilities. Automatic Network Routing (ARN) is the layer 3 protocol. Like IP, it does not do any error checking or packet resequencing. However, there are many differences between IP and ARN. We will discuss HPR (RTP and ANR) in a few moments.

APPN: Flow Control

123

APPN: Flow Control

- Adaptive rate based (ARB)
    - Preventive flow control mechanism

- HPR boundary function

- Coexistence with APPN / ISR nodes

HPR uses an innovative flow control mechanism, Adaptive Rate Based (ABR) protocol, which is a preventive flow control mechanism. The mechanism is designed to predict network congestion and takes steps to ensure it does not occur. The algorithm monitors incoming and outgoing transmission rates. Measurements taken are recorded based on the time it takes to get responses from remote nodes. As the time of the responses increases, the node predicts congestion and reduces the flow of traffic between those nodes.

HPR also defines a boundary function that allows for interconnection of SNA networks. Legacy SNA networks have the ability to connect different networks together using a set of protocols called SNI (SNA Network Interconnection). The HPR boundary function provides similar support by using a special type of NN. The boundary NN provides a gateway from one SNA APPN to another. HPR is also designed to coexist with the older APPN ISR nodes, since most SNA APPN devices originally used ISR.

124

APPN: Automatic Network Routing (ANR)

APPN: Automatic Network
Routing (ANR)

- Reroute capabilities with session failure
- Fast forwarding rate
- Minimum network resources required
  - CPU
  - Memory

ANR was designed to have extremely low latency and uses a label-swapping technique similar to source route bridging. So, while IP examines an incoming packet's address and dynamically forwards it to the current next-hop router, ANR uses a static label contained in each packet that has local significance to the forwarding ANR router. Once the packet is forwarded, the ANR router will remove its portion of the header. This is a very simple forwarding mechanism that does not require table lookups or complex code to implement. The router labels are determined when the SNA session starts and remain in effect until the session is terminated. ANR cannot reroute packets around a failed link or router. It relies on HPR to establish the path across the network and provide error detection and correction.

APPN: Rapid Transport Protocol

> ## APPN: Rapid Transport Protocol
> - Connection-oriented transport
>   - Similar to TCP, OSI Class 4 transport level
> - End-to-end error recovery
> - Segmentation/reassembly

The layer 4 reliable connection is based on RTP, or Rapid Transport Protocol. It is a connection-oriented protocol that runs in the end points of the APPN network. It provides all error recovery, retransmission of packets, and packet sequencing.

While RTP has some functions similar to TCP, there are quite a few differences. RTP is responsible for route calculation, removing that burden from the intermediate nodes within an APPN network. At session establishment, RTP builds a list of labels that have local sig-

nificance to the intermediate NNs. These labels are prefixed in the APPN header, which provides the entire routing path.

RTP establishes a session with an RTP device (RTP partners). RTP can detect when it is not communicating with its partner. In this case, RTP will determine if there is another path acceptable for this level of service. Assuming there is an alternate path, RTP will then establish the best route to use. This occurs without disrupting the session between its RTP components.

126

APPN: Nodes

This slide shows how APPN sessions are established across the network. Note that it also illustrates the ability to integrate ISR traffic into an HPR network. The CP session is established between network nodes and also between the network node and the end node. ISR routing is used between end node A and network node B. An RTP connection is built between network nodes B and D. CP sessions are established between each of the adjacent nodes. In this case, an ISR node initiates a session from network node A. NNB terminates the ISR session and forwards the information to EN D using HPR .

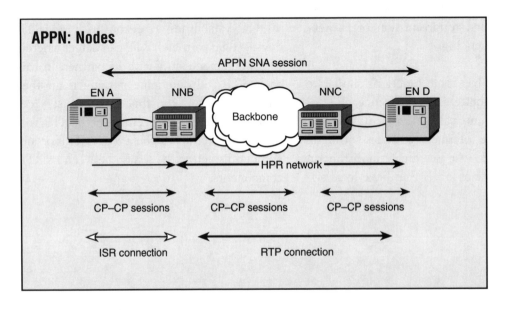

APPN: Services

> **APPN: Services**
>
> - APPN dynamic resource registration locates the applications
> - Topology and routing services
> - Network management
> - Dependent LU requester/server (DLUR/S) preserves clients' devices and applications
> - Future native ATM DLC maps CoS to QoS

APPN offers a variety of services to network users. These include the ability to perform directory searches, register end node LU resources, a robust priority scheme (Class of Service), topology and routing services, and session services. Network management services include traditional legacy management services based on Netview (NMVT) and SNMP network management.

A powerful feature of APPN is the ability of ENs to dynamically register applications or logical units. This provides the APPN network with the capability of building a directory of all user applications and LUs. APPN networks can locate applications including the ability to dynamically locate applications that may move from one host to another. The network automatically discovers the location of any device, application, or any other network resource.

In order to support legacy SNA information, APPN has functions called the Dependent LU Requester (DLUR) and the Dependent LU Server (DLUS). These APPN applications preserve communications between traditional or legacy SNA devices across an APPN network.

128 APPN: Dependent LU Requester (DLUR)

Dependent LU Requester (DLUR) is an application that resides in either an end node or network node. Its propose is to provide a transport for legacy SNA traffic across an SNA network. An example of an end node is a 3174 controller, while a network node might be a router. DLUR functions to support legacy LU types (dependent LU0, 1, 2, 3). This type of traffic is destined for a legacy SNA application on a mainframe. DLUR requires a DLUS (Dependent LU Server) application on the mainframe.

DLUS is the "partner" application to DLUR. Like DLUR, it is an APPN application that is used to support legacy SNA traffic across an APPN network. It is only supported by VTAM and will execute only on an SNA mainframe. DLUS requires a remote DLUR application. It was first implemented in VTAM version 4.2. IBM built this to facilitate the adoption of APPN, since APPN cannot natively transport or handle legacy SNA protocols. Legacy SNA control and management flows are encapsulated in LU6.2 sessions, which support the SSCP-to-PU and SSCP-to-LU sessions. DLUR natively transports the LU data using either ISR or HPR. DLUS's function on the mainframe is to support the SSCP-to-PU and LU flows and direct the delivery of the native LU traffic to the appropriate legacy application.

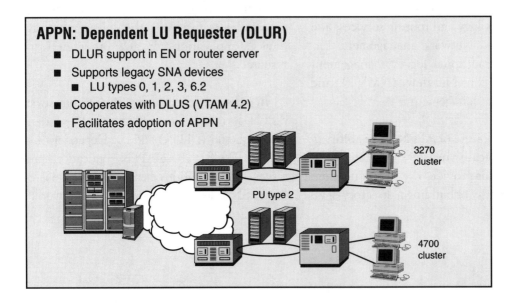

APPN: Dependent LU Requester (DLUR)
- DLUR support in EN or router server
- Supports legacy SNA devices
  - LU types 0, 1, 2, 3, 6.2
- Cooperates with DLUS (VTAM 4.2)
- Facilitates adoption of APPN

PU type 2

3270 cluster

4700 cluster

APPN was developed to support peer-to-peer communications following a client/server model. It is based on the TCP/IP model (layer 3 connectionless routing ANR and layer 4 reliability RTP). It also has advanced features like application registration and extensive flow control.

APPN has a robust class of service (CoS) that can be mapped to an ATM QoS. In this manner, APPN has the ability to request and reserve specific bandwidth for applications. HPR's highly efficient routing mechanism provides for the integration of voice and video applications within the APPN datagram. ABR congestion management was designed for optimal control with gigabit-speed networks. This combination of performance, reliability, and network traffic control is designed for today's multimedia applications and the integration of voice, video, and data.

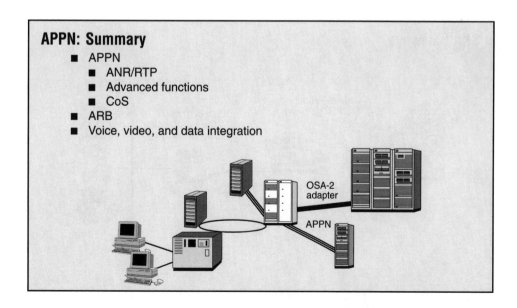

APPN: Summary
- APPN
  - ANR/RTP
  - Advanced functions
  - CoS
- ARB
- Voice, video, and data integration

SNA Gateways

There are several other techniques to integrate SNA traffic across your company's intranet. These include encapsulating SNA and using gateway services. One of the earlier more popular gateway services was Novell Systems' SAA IPX gateway. A second solution is using TN3270 or TN3270(E) gateways, and the final and emerging technology is using Web browsers.

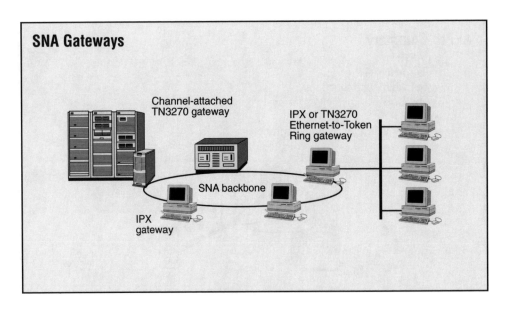

SNA Gateways

Channel-attached TN3270 gateway

IPX or TN3270 Ethernet-to-Token Ring gateway

SNA backbone

IPX gateway

SNA Gateways: SAA and IPX

A very common SNA integration technique is using Novell's SAA gateways. Remote workstations connect to a central site SAA gateway. The remote workstation uses IPX client software and native IPX routing throughout the WAN. The gateway converts the IPX data frame to a native SNA data frame. The remote IPX SSA client appears as an LU to the mainframe, serviced by the PU defined in the SAA gateway.

This integrates SNA traffic into a WAN using IPX as a routable software and providing SNA connectivity to users who have IPX client software. It is limited to only devices that specifically support Novell SAA gateways. It does not provide any connectivity support for Legacy 3270 controllers that may exist within the network. Also, typically, the gateways are not channel attached, so one of the channel-attached gateways we discussed earlier is needed to connect to the mainframe.

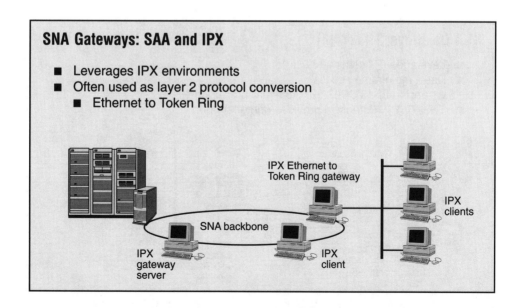

SNA Gateways: SAA and IPX

- Leverages IPX environments
- Often used as layer 2 protocol conversion
  - Ethernet to Token Ring

IPX Ethernet to Token Ring gateway

SNA backbone

IPX clients

IPX gateway server

IPX client

TN3270 is rapidly becoming a very popular integration technique. It uses a native TCP/IP communications stack and is a hybrid of TCP/IP telnet software specially designed to handle SNA 3270 datastreams. TN3270 or TN3270(E) (a modified version of the original TN3270 specification that provides support for an attached workstation printer) allows users to connect directly to a mainframe and access native SNA 3270 applications. This of course assumes that the mainframe has a channel connection that supports native TCP/IP traffic and TCP/IP software executing on the mainframe along with TN3270(E) server software.

Though TCP software is becoming more popular on the mainframe, there are still users who do not want to introduce another channel-attached device or want to incur the overhead of running TCP/IP and TN3270 client software on their mainframe. For these users, a remote gateway can be used to support TN3270 server software and convert the TN3270 stream into a native SNA stream. This is similar to the SAA gateway environment. The major differences are that almost any standard TN3270 client software works with TN3270 gateways, and IP is used instead of IPX as the network protocol. In addition, LAN-attached 3174s also support TN3270 sessions from a LAN interface. A 3174 controller with the proper microcode allows each of the coax terminals to establish a telnet session to the mainframe or one of these gateways, thus

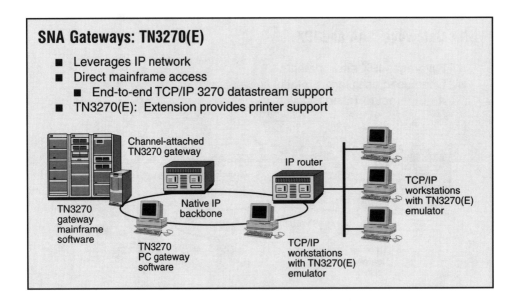

SNA Gateways: TN3270(E)

- Leverages IP network
- Direct mainframe access
  - End-to-end TCP/IP 3270 datastream support
- TN3270(E): Extension provides printer support

Channel-attached TN3270 gateway

IP router

TN3270 gateway mainframe software

Native IP backbone

TN3270 PC gateway software

TCP/IP workstations with TN3270(E) emulator

TCP/IP workstations with TN3270(E) emulator

providing native IP services directly from that device. Also channel-attaching the TN3270 gateways is becoming very popular Channel attaching these gateways simplify the network's design, and the better ones also provide native SNA and TCP/IP access to the mainframe.

A major flaw in this integration is that it does not provide support for SDLC-attached controllers, so the older legacy devices cannot be incorporated using these techniques. It does, however, give us the flexibility to either use a host-based software or to offload the mainframe with TN3270 and set up either a LAN-attached or channel-attached gateway.

133

SNA Gateways: Web Browser Support TN3270(E)

Web browser support is rapidly becoming the preferred way to support SNA applications. Its primary advantages are software distribution and control, and it is very easy to use. It is actually a TN3270(E) application that is much easier to control and access by an end user. A typical user, using his or her Web-based browser, connects to a server/gateway. The gateway downloads a TN3270(E) application, typically a Java applet, to the workstation. The workstation then brings up a 3270 green screen session with basic 3270 functionality to the mainframe. Web server applications are emerging on the mainframe, as well as PC- and channel-attached gateway devices. The ease-of-use features of browser technology and central control of the emulator (no PC software to buy and install/maintain on the workstations) makes it very attractive to both network designers and users.

TN3270(E), of course, also has its problems. There is no support for legacy controllers. Additionally, the PC must support browser and Java applets, something older devices may not provide.

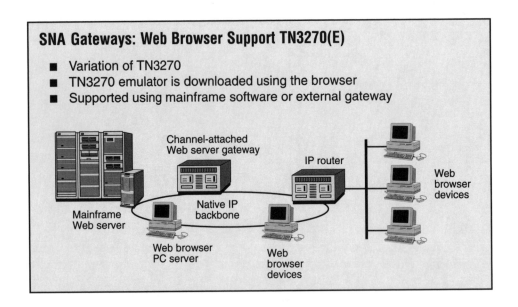

SNA Gateways: Web Browser Support TN3270(E)

- Variation of TN3270
- TN3270 emulator is downloaded using the browser
- Supported using mainframe software or external gateway

SNA Gateways: Summary

134

We have explored the arguably simplest form of SNA integration. Gateway technology allows an end user to deliver an SNA transaction in a native TCP/IP or IPX routable frame. To support this technology, we need to use any of the available software products that provide an endstation with TN3270(E) functionality. (Note that the E in TN3270(E) provides for multiple LU support. This is typically used to support PC-attached printers.)

These emulators require a TN3270 server. The server can be software installed on the mainframe (which would require the mainframe to support TCP/IP). Another option is to offload TCP/IP software and the TN3270(E) server support from the mainframe and use an external gateway. These gateways can be LAN attached and leverage the existing legacy channel-attached gateways. The servers can also be channel attached, eliminating the need for the legacy channel gateway. Web server technology is an extenuation of the 3270(E) support. Instead of maintaining, installing, and purchasing TN3270 software for the enterprise workstations, the workstations can use their Web browsers to download Java TN3270(E) applets. This allows the enterprise to eliminate the cost of installing, maintaining, and purchasing an emulator for each device in the network. The software is supported on the server, the licensing charge is based on concurrent access, and, most importantly, users can access the mainframe with a familiar and easy-to-use browser.

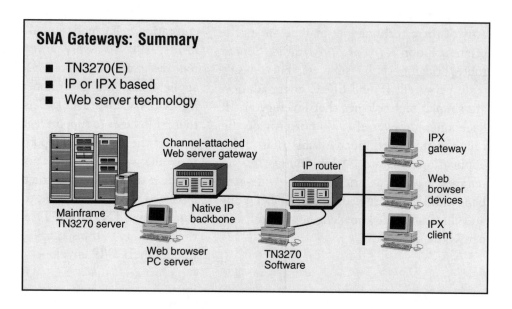

SNA Gateways: Summary

- TN3270(E)
- IP or IPX based
- Web server technology

135

SNA Summary and Recommendations

SNA Summary and Recommendations

- Bridging
  - Source route
  - Transparent or source route transparent
- IP encapsulation
- SDLC pass-through
- Datalink switching
  - Frame relay
- APPN: Client/server SNA protocol suite
- Network gateways
  - TN3270(E), IPX SAA

We've studied the various SNA integration technologies. We've covered their operation, benefits, and the issues they pose to the network manager and designer. Any of these technologies may be an appropriate solution for your SNA traffic. Source route bridging is the simplest, but doesn't scale very well. IP and SDLC encapsulation are simpler technologies that leverage an IP backbone; however, they do not provide the reliable transport mechanisms that SNA applications require. Additionally, session outages may occur and valuable wide-area bandwidth is consumed, since SDLC polls and LLC2 RR acknowledgments are sent across the network.

Datalink switching and frame relay RFC 1490 solve problems that SRB, IP, and SDLC encapsulation present. They reliably transport SNA traffic across the network and remove endstation SDLC polls and LLC2 acknowledgments. APPN is a very powerful protocol, but was designed to support SNA client/server applications, and does not natively support legacy SNA flows. DLUS/R is the mechanism that APPN uses to support legacy SNA. APPN requires the enterprise support of a second protocol along with IP. It does not take advantage of the existing IP infrastructure. We've also discussed native IP network transport for 3270 datastreams. TN3270 or TN3270(E) provides the capability to transport SNA 3270 information in an TCP/IP envelope.

Part Eight

SNA Summary and Conclusions

Technology Solutions

136

> ## Technology Solutions
>
> - Legacy technologies
>   - Source route bridging
>   - IP and SDLC encapsulation
>
> - Contemporary solutions
>   - DLSw and SNA frame relay (RFC 1490)
>   - APPN
>
> - Gateway solutions
>   - IPX gateway
>   - TN3270(E) and Web browser

We can break down the technologies that you have read about into three basic categories: The first we can categorize as *legacy solutions*. Included in this group are source route bridging, SDLC encapsulation, and IP encapsulation. (IP encapsulation is LAN encapsulation of MAC frames.) The second category is *contemporary solutions*. This category includes DLSw, RFC 1490 (both BNN and BAN), and, of course, APPN. The third and final category is *gateway solutions*. This category involves passing native SNA over IP. The techniques include using gateways or direct mainframe accesses supporting TN3270 or TN3270(E), and Web browser sessions. These techniques allow native SNA traffic to be transported with TCP/IP datagrams directly from the originating workstation right to the mainframe. They are clearly the simplest ways to get data from one point to another.

As described earlier, there are three proto-cols: SRB, SDLC encapsulation, and IP encapsulation. Let's look at each one in more detail. Source route bridging, or SRB, is clearly the simplest and quickest way to transport SNA packets across the network. The processing cycles used in the various bridges of the network are the lowest, and they contain the least amount of packet overhead as compared to any of the other techniques. These are two basic and major advantages of source route bridging.

However, SRB does come with some problems. The first, as described earlier, is that SRB uses LLC2 to encapsulate the SNA frames. LLC2, or Logical Link Control 2, provides reli-able transport of the SNA frames between the two SNA endstations. It uses timers (T1 and Ti) that have to be acknowledged within a finite period of time. The LLC2 acknowledg-ment frames generate additional overhead across the network. This takes up bandwidth over wide-area links. Also, the timers have low values (they were designed to work over LAN connections), so they have the propensity to time-out by crossing slower-speed WAN con-nections, especially if the WAN is having a moment of congestion. This can result in ses-sion time-outs during which sessions are termi-nated and users are forced to log on to their SNA host. Bridging is also subject to broadcast storms. When an SNA endstation wants to discover its partner, it issues a broadcast. In the

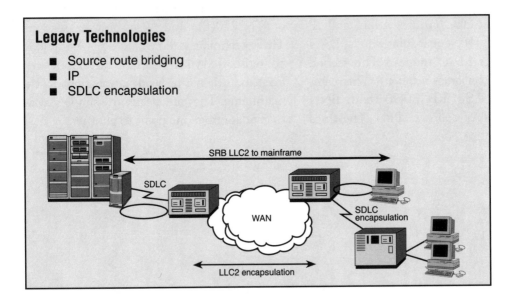

Legacy Technologies

- Source route bridging
- IP
- SDLC encapsulation

SRB LLC2 to mainframe

SDLC

WAN

SDLC encapsulation

LLC2 encapsulation

source route bridge network this is propagated throughout the entire network and can greatly increase the amount of traffic over your WANs as well as your LANs. One of the largest problems today with SNA is the fact that there are no reroute capabilities using SRB. As SNA sessions are built using source route bridging, a specific routing field is defined called the Routing Information Field, part of the Token Ring or Token Ring MAC frame. This information field has all of the route information that a packet needs. If one of those intermediate bridges or LANs fail, the packet cannot be routed, and the session fails, forcing the SNA user to again log on to the host, assuming that there is an alternate path available.

The second legacy technology is SDLC encapsulation. It is used to support the oldest of the SNA devices. These may include Physical Unit Type 1 devices, which today are more common in AS/400s. Unfortunately, this protocol has many more problems than benefits. There is no local acknowledgment of the SDLC polls, causing all polls to be transmitted across the network. This generates significantly more overhead across the network since each poll has to be encapsulated. It also increases the propensity for SNA session timeouts. Since each poll is encapsulated and sent across the network, a congested network link may cause a delay or drop a poll. When a poll is missed, the endstations enter into a recovery state, and sessions can fail. Also, there is no reliable transport of this information. SDLC encapsulation uses connectionless protocols and does not guarantee delivery between the

SDLC stations. Last, and one of the largest problems, is the fact that it does not scale; typically, SDLC encapsulation does not support multidrop capabilities. So, in an enterprise with 500 remote locations, each with an SDLC connection, 500 router ports are required at the central site. More importantly, 500 FEP ports are also required, making this a very expensive and nonscalable solution.

The third legacy technology is IP encapsulation, which is similar to SDLC encapsulation. The difference is that IP encapsulation specifically applies to Token Ring LAN interfaces. The benefits include broadcast reductions, since frames are specifically sent to a destination Token Ring. A single protocol (IP) is used across the network. This allows you to more easily maintain and troubleshoot your WAN.

Our example uses a LAN-attached Token Ring 3174 or a PC. These devices send a datagram to the LAN interface on the router. The router then takes the entire MAC frame and encapsulates it in an IP and UDP header. This new packet is then sent across the network until it is received by its destination router. The destination router de-encapsulates the IP and UDP datagram and delivers the MAC frame on its local ring. A major benefit is that the entire IP network appears as a single source route bridge hop, taking up a single entry in the RIF field. This can drastically increase the available hops a packet can cross.

IP encapsulation is not without its problems. It has no reliable delivery of SNA traffic, so as the network becomes congested causing routers to drop packets because of link issues, or packets get delayed because of overloaded links, the SNA traffic can easily time-out. This can result in lost SNA sessions and force users to log back on to their mainframe applications. In addition, LLC2 overhead traffic is transported across the network. This can greatly increase the overhead on WAN links, consuming its bandwidth.

DLSw is the most popular solution in this group and uses an enveloping technique versus an encapsulation technique. Remember, enveloping drops the layer 2 frames and processes the native SNA traffic by inserting it in a TCP/IP datagram. Some of the benefits of DLSw are reduced broadcasts (eliminates traffic), local acknowledgment (reduces traffic and eliminate session time-outs), reroutability (IP), and reliability (TCP).

Traffic is reduced since broadcasts are directed to a point in the network and all the LLC2 acknowledgments do not have to cross the WAN. The time-outs are eliminated because the SDLC and LAN interfaces immediately receive acknowledgment after frames are either sent or received. Since sessions do not time-out, the stability and reliability of the network is also increased. SNA can also be rerouted around failed devices or links since it is using IP, while TCP provides the same reliable transport that native SNA users are used to receiving.

There are some concerns about DLSw scaling to support large networks. However, scaling issues are not a major factor because of code maturity (DLSw has been available for over four years) and the processing power and memory of today's routers. Several years ago, the processing power available within the industry was significantly less than today's, causing a much bigger concern. Consider that routers were based on 286 or 386 SX type CPUs, which

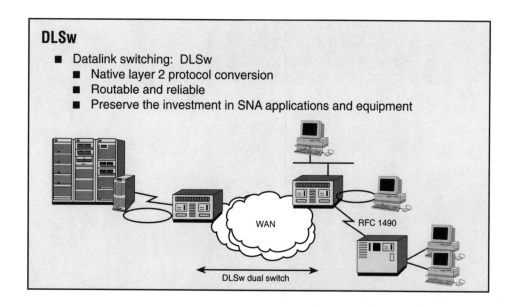

DLSw
- Datalink switching: DLSw
  - Native layer 2 protocol conversion
  - Routable and reliable
  - Preserve the investment in SNA applications and equipment

WAN

RFC 1490

DLSw dual switch

were state-of-the-art systems. Today, we have gone to Pentium II and RISC-based processors. Older routers typically had 4 or 8 megabytes of memory—not much, considering everything they needed to do. Today, many systems contain 16, 32, and sometimes even 64 megabytes of memory, with the largest systems having in excess of 800 megabytes available. This technology jump, along with code improvements and maturity, has allowed very large scalable DLSw networks to emerge. Also, more current versions of DLSw, specifically, RFC 2166, address some scaling issues and also reduce the TCP sessions.

Another major concern is the overhead involved in transporting DLSw traffic across a network. DLSw uses TCP/IP (which adds 40 bytes to the native SNA datagram) and SSP (which adds an additional 16 bytes). However, remember that DLSw envelops SNA and does not encapsulate. So, when transporting SNA frames from a Token Ring environment, DLSw eliminates the Token Ring MAC frame and Logical Link Control 2 framing. Combining this should reduce the DLSw overhead figure of 56 bytes by at least 23 bytes (as a result of eliminating the 802.5 MAC header, some minimal RIF information, and LLC2 control fields). In addition, since DLSw responds to LLC2 RR polls, they are not transported across the network. This should save another 23+ bytes per response.

Boundary Access Node (BAN) and Boundary Network Node (BNN) use frame relay and RFC 1490 to transport SNA across a WAN. As we discussed earlier, RFC 1490 defines the method to transport data between two frame relay-attached devices. When transmitting SNA, it provides a very simple solution, appearing as a bridged network.

Frame relay implements a single-switch datalink switch at the remote locations. SNA traffic generated at a remote location is locally acknowledged (LLC2 termination and acknowledgment) and then enveloped using a technique similar to DLSw. Instead of enveloping the SNA datagram in a TCP/IP and SSP header, a RFC 1490 frame relay is

generated. This package includes a LLC2 header (BNN), an LLC2 and Token Ring MAC header (BAN), and the native SNA frame (TH/RH/RU). The frame size for BAN is at least 25 bytes and 10 bytes for BNN (excluding link-level framing). In addition, both these implementations use LLC2 between the routes; therefore, additional overhead is created for LLC2 RR acknowledgments and keep-alive frames. Be careful of proponents who claim RFC 1490 is preferred because of its lower overhead. They often do not consider the LLC2 acknowledgments in their overhead calculations. Also, be careful about increasing the LLC2 window size. This can cause a massive amount of retransmitted data if a packet is lost.

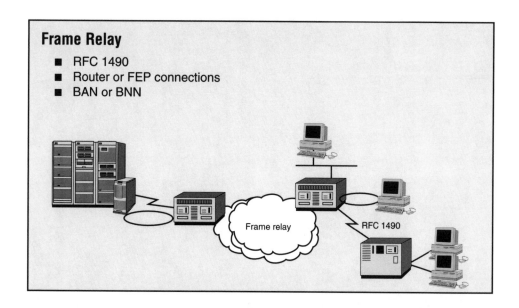

Frame Relay
- RFC 1490
- Router or FEP connections
- BAN or BNN

Frame relay

RFC 1490

RFC 1490 is limited to a design that requires logical point-to-point frame relay connections. As intermediate routers are introduced within the network, RFC 1490 limitations are magnified, and it can become difficult to use.

Also, frame relay BAN and BNN do not support reroute capabilities. Consider the frame relay "cloud." There is at least a point-to-point circuit between the remote frame relay FRAD and the central site router. If that PVC fails, frame relay cannot reroute traffic around the failure. The frame relay FRAD does not possess knowledge about the topology to reroute across another PVC.

140

APPN is one my of favorite protocols. It is an elegant solution that supports client/server-based applications. Its architecture is very similar to TCP/IP, with several "advanced" features. APPN High-Performance Routing (HPR) uses two protocols: Rapid Transport Protocol (RTP) is a layer 4 transport protocol, and Automatic Network Routing (ANR is a layer 3 network protocol. RTP is similar to TCP, providing a reliable connection between the endstations. ANR, like IP, is a connectionless protocol, but, unlike IP, it implements a source route bridge-like transport method with locally significant labels. This method provides a very efficient transport for information throughout the network.

APPN is an excellent solution for native SNA client/server traffic based on LU6.2. DLUR and DLUS provide an excellent solution for transporting native SNA legacy traffic; legacy SNA traffic is converted to APPN labels and forwarded throughout the network.

The biggest concern about APPN is its lack of acceptance within the industry. While it may be the most elegant technology, there is very little industry knowledge or expertise in designing, implementing, and supporting APPN networks. It forces the enterprise customer to build a multiprotocol network. Today's trend in networking is to reduce protocols, and IP seems to have won this battle. IP

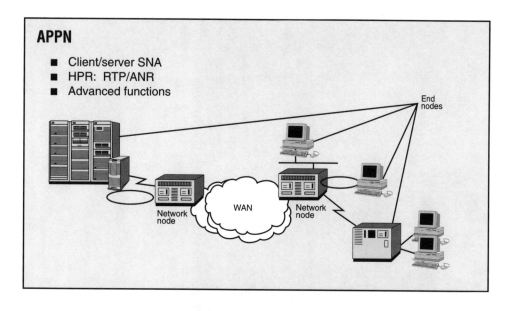

APPN

- Client/server SNA
- HPR: RTP/ANR
- Advanced functions

End nodes

Network node

WAN

Network node

networks also offer good integration techniques to transport SNA information.

A variation of APPN is starting to gain in popularity. It is called HPR over IP. It has the advantage of using IP as the layer 3 transport, which allows it to leverage an IP infrastructure. It will be interesting to watch how the industry views and accepts this technology.

TN3270 and TN3270(E), along with Web browser support, are available today and rapidly growing in popularity. A workstation with a TCP/IP stack and TN3270(E) emulator uses a native end-to-end IP transport across the WAN and LAN. This provides the network manager with an easy, single-protocol network to manage. The SNA data uses TCP/IP within a specialized telnet session that supports 3270 datastreams. The E extension provides additional LU support for locally attached printers.

A major advantage of TN3270 is that a variety of emulators can be used. A specific client/server emulator package to support SNA is not required. You can use TN3270 to connect directly to the mainframe or a local TN3270 gateway server. Also, since the 3174s support TN3270 using a LAN attachment, your traditional 3270 coax terminals can also use this solution. This 3174 feature allows 3174 coax-attached terminals to telnet using TN3270 into an IBM host or gateway server and to receive the same SNA 3270 screen capabilities they would as if they were using native SNA protocols.

Web browser support is another technique rapidly increasing in popularity. Its benefits include ease of use and central-site software control. It is easy to use because users only need to know how to access a browser to gain mainframe sessions. A user connects to either

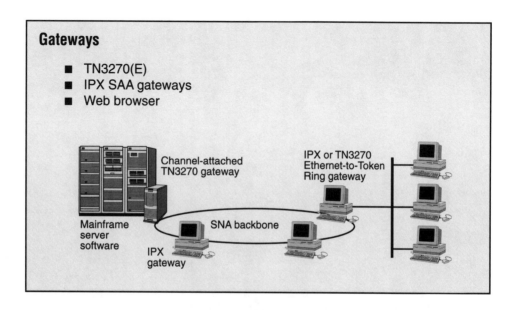

Gateways

- TN3270(E)
- IPX SAA gateways
- Web browser

Channel-attached TN3270 gateway

IPX or TN3270 Ethernet-to-Token Ring gateway

Mainframe server software

SNA backbone

IPX gateway

an SNA Web server gateway or Web server software on the mainframe. A Java applet is downloaded to the workstation and allows the user to bring up a 3270 session to the host.

In addition to its usability characteristics, an enterprise can also easily upgrade emulators by changing the software on the Web server. Also, since the software is located on the server, an enterprise can also save a considerable amount of PC software. Emulators do not have to be purchased and installed on each PC; instead, a site pays for a concurrent license charge.

Now that we have looked at the options for integrating your SNA traffic into your TCP/IP intranet, we need to determine which is the "right" one to use. Consider extending the 7-layer OSI communication model to include layers 8, 9, and 10. These layers are Financial, Political, and Religious.

These personal biases come into play whenever a decision is made. Selecting the best financial decisions is always critical for your organization. Financial decisions typically consider the cost of communications and facilities. However, you should also consider the cost of supporting your network, managing it, and the cost to your business if the network fails. The religious and political considerations revolve around the culture and comfort with a solution. Since most of the solutions we presented are good, an enterprise should consider what it "feels comfortable learning and supporting." If the enterprise is comfortable with source route bridging, then this may be an acceptable solution. In fact, all the technologies that we spoke about are acceptable. You need to consider the size of your network, and the frequency and size of your datagrams. We discussed the pro and cons of these solutions, so you can make the best educated decisions based on the facts.

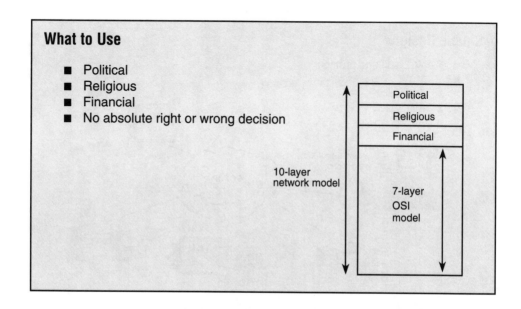

What to Use

- Political
- Religious
- Financial
- No absolute right or wrong decision

Political

Religious

Financial

10-layer network model

7-layer OSI model

143 Simple Design

As a former operator, systems programmer, network designer, and systems engineer, I have learned the best solution is also the simplest. Simple solutions result in the easiest networks to maintain and expand.

Let's start by considering the goals of our network design. First, there are tremendous benefits in selecting a single protocol for the backbone. A single protocol allows uniform management and troubleshooting of problems. A common set of tools and expertise reduces both the number of engineers needed to support an enterprise and the amount of network downtime due to a problem. Both these result in lower overall costs for your business.

The second consideration is to provide your customers the same level (or better!) of network performance and access. The single protocol, legacy host-centric environment provides the network designer the ability to monitor and manage the network. In the host-centric world, the enterprise is able to understand the end users' traffic patterns and tendencies, making it possible to determine and set the end users' network performance expectations by using a variety of tuning mechanisms. The end users' expectations can be set and met by the network planners.

These host-centric environments are rapidly becoming obsolete as organizations need to

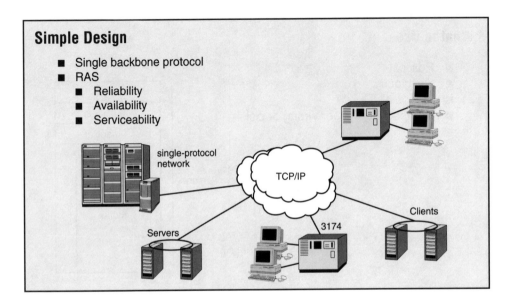

access a variety of resources in different locations. Yet we still need to preserve the characteristics of the host-centric environment by maintaining and improving on RAS: Reliability, Availability, and Serviceability.

144 TN3270 and DLSw

Considering these requirements, we should select technologies that preserve 3270 applications while providing the simplest integration. Web browser technology provides users with the easiest navigation tools and a common look and feel of their PCs. The software is installed and maintained at the central site. This offers easier control to upgrade and troubleshoot user problems. It also ensures that each user is using the most current supported version of the emulator software. Costs are typically reduced, since the end user does not need to purchase a software product; typically, these products have a "seat" charge. This allows the enterprise to pay a license fee for each concurrent user, instead of a fee for each device.

If your site already has a TCP/IP software package that includes a TN3270 emulator, adding a TN3270 server is a similar solution without the expense of upgrading or adding a Web server. You may need to add a central site TN3270 server. Both the Web server and TN3270 server come in a variety of options. These include a direct pass-through connection to the mainframe's TCP/IP software. In this solution, the mainframe needs to be upgraded to run TCP/IP. A standalone PC or Unix server can be installed. This has the benefit of providing minimal disruption to the mainframe and leverages the existing SNA channel-attached gateway. It is also typically the lowest-cost solution. Finally, a channel-attached server gateway can be purchased.

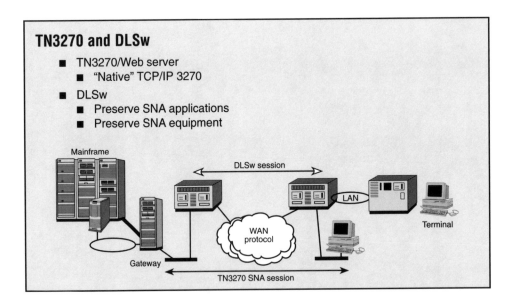

TN3270 and DLSw
- TN3270/Web server
  - "Native" TCP/IP 3270
- DLSw
  - Preserve SNA applications
  - Preserve SNA equipment

This has the benefit of replacing the existing and sometimes very expensive SNA FEPs. It also provides support for end-to-end TCP/IP SNA integration across the network, while maintaining a SNA host. It accomplishes this by supporting a TCP/IP TN3270 session over the WAN and LAN and converts this session to a native SNA session across the channel.

Both the TN3270 and Web server option provide simplest SNA integration. They preserve the SNA 3270 application and data-stream, while leveraging an end-to-end IP network environment.

However, not every device in your network is a PC. For devices that cannot use this technology, I strongly recommend the use of DLSw. DLSw is an industry-wide accepted protocol. It has the ability to scale into a very large network, provides a native TCP/IP

transport across the network, and still gives SNA a reliable mechanism to transport SNA. Almost any SNA device using a variety of media types is supported by DLSw. This includes Token Ring, Ethernet, FDDI, X.25, frame relay, and of course, SDLC-attached devices. It preserves the investment in equipment and most importantly, the investment in SNA 3270 legacy applications. Since DLSw supports PU2.1, it is also a solution to support APPN devices across an IP intranet. DLSw provides the network designer the flexibility of developing APPN applications and still use a single-protocol IP backbone.

The combination of Web browser technology, TN3270 access, and DLSw provides a high-performance, easy-to-implement-and-manage network. These technologies allow your enterprise environment to integrate SNA traffic into your TCP/IP enterprise intranet.

Appendix

DLSw Configuration Notes

145

DLSw Installation

- Just another protocol
- Unique design considerations
  - Multiple protocol support
  - Memory calculations
- Identify "key" parameters

A DLSw installation can be complex. Many problems often result in the fact that DLSw technology is not sufficiently understood. This should no longer be your problem. Remember the three protocols that DLSw uses: source route bridging, TCP/IP, and SSP. The good news is that you really have nothing to configure with SSP, which leaves you to configure your TCP/IP and SRB in Token Ring environments. You will need to configure SRB only on Token Ring LAN interfaces. The key to flawless DLSw implementation is *planning*. DLSw networks must be well planned and designed. Also, remember that I described DLSw as an application. This simply means that if your IP network is not working well, neither will DLSw. In fact, that leads me to my first piece of advice: Never try to turn on a remote location with DLSw and IP, and for

that matter any other protocols, at the same time. I have seen many situations in which time is spent troubleshooting DLSw problems while, in fact, the IP network is not working well or the links between the routers are not working well. Therefore, much of the problem determination efforts are usually or typically misdirected. I strongly recommend that you first have a working IP network. You should be able to reliably telnet and manage each router within the network.

After the IP network is working to your satisfaction, you can now go about configuring DLSw. Remember, the most important point is *planning*.

DLSw is just another protocol; however, it does have unique design considerations. Since it is an application, you need to understand how other protocols are going to affect it. Identify key memory and CPU calculations from your router vendor in order to support the desired number of SNA PUs and TCP connections. This is especially important at the central site to which all your remote devices will connect. If you have many PUs or your remote routers need to connect to several DLSw peers, make sure that you understand the remote routers' CPU and memory calculations. Next, I'll give you some key parameters that you need to identify.

DLSw Parameters

> **DLSw Parameters**
>
> - Global
>   - Virtual ring ID
>
> - Peer address
>   - Address of remote router
>   - Recommend connectionless or slot address
>
> - SAP table
>   - Defaults 00,04,08,0C
>   - Usually OK, 04 the most popular

DLSw has several parameters that you need to identify. The first one is normally a global ring number. This allows DLSw to terminate RIFs, and to determine if packets are coming in from another DLSw router so that broadcasts are not looped within the network. Remember, DLSw and Token Ring environments use source route bridging, so by identifying a common virtual ring number for DLSw, it stops loops within your network. A second parameter is typically a peer address. These are addresses that you need to provide your routers so that TCP sessions and/or broadcasts can be directed to the proper routers. These are typically configured in a remote router that points to the central site router. You need to identify the IP address(es) of the central site router(s) and configure it as a peer in each remote.

You must also configure the SAPs that are going to be DLSw. The most common SNA SAPs are 00, 04, 08, and 0C. Most SNA devices use these SAPs and vendors may include them as default DLSw SAPs. Remember this if you encounter an SNA that cannot make a connection over a DLSw network: Check its SNA SAP. If it is using a SAP that is not defined to DLSw, the device will not be switched across the network.

When you define DLSw on a Token Ring interface, you will configure source route bridging on the interface. Do not worry, SRB is *not* configured across the WAN. You should always plan the SRB network by determining the various ring numbers on both sides of the network and any other router vendor-specific parameters that may be required. It is best to lay out a diagram of what your ring numbers will be and also decide whether you want all your remote ring numbers to be the same or unique within the network. This is possible in the DLSw environment, since bridging *only* exists on the Token Ring interface and the SRB RIF is terminated by DLSw.

Typically, you need to identify a global ring number and a virtual ring number within that particular router. Remember from our discussion of source route bridging, all multiport bridges bridge from an interface to an internal ring number, so make sure both of those are defined and configured.

DLSw SDLC Parameters

- Poll address: Defined in the controller and/or NCP

- NRZ/NRZI: Defined in controller and/or NCP

- MAXDATA: Defined in controller and/or NCP and/or VTAM

- Source MAC: Unique LAA you make up

- Destination MAC: Gateway address (3745,3172,AS/400)

- IDBLK: Defined in VTAM

- IDNUM: Defined in VTAM

When defining a remote SDLC controller, there are several line or link parameters that have to be defined to the router that are typically defined in the front-end processor or the NCP. The first parameter is the poll address, which must match the controller configuration. The poll address is the specific SDLC address that the controller responds. Another parameter is the line encoding technique: NRZ or NRZI. This is also defined in the controller and the NCP. Again, you must configure the router to match controller configuration.

The MAXDATA parameter defines the amount of information that can be transmitted between the router and the controller. This is an important parameter, because if it is set incorrectly, you could overrun the buffers in the controller. A remote SDLC device that is datalink switched will typically connect to a LAN interface at the central site. LAN interfaces default to larger MAXDATA sizes. In order eliminate performance problems and connectivity issues, make sure the MAXDATA parameter on the host's LAN interface matches that on the controller and router. This is either 265 (for older controllers) or 521.

You will need to identify a unique source MAC address for the SDLC controller. This is only known to the router. Since DLSw is converting between layer 2 protocols (in most cases, from SDLC to Token Ring), the router needs to present a unique MAC address to the host on behalf of the controller. Of course, you will also need a destination gateway MAC address, which is the address of the SNA gateway (in LAN environments). This gateway address is your channel-attached SNA gateway.

Finally, if you are using either a FEP or one of the gateways that use host-based switch-line protocols (3172 or channel-attached router), you need to identify the ID BLOCK and IDNUM parameters. These parameters should be supplied to you by your VTAM systems programmer.

This is a universal worksheet that allows you to identify many of the planning parameters required to install DLSw. If you can fill out most of these parameters, you should be able to complete a DLSw installation with minimal problems.

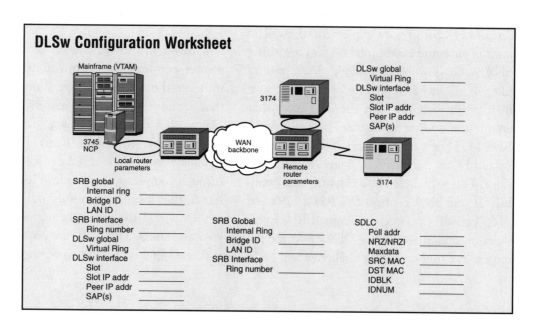

DLSw Configuration Worksheet

DLSw Performance, Priority

DLSw Performance, Priority

- Filters
  - Protocol priority
    - Set the DLSw ports 2065–2067 to high-priority queue
  - DLSw priority
    - Filter on MAC, SAP, or any field in TH/RH/RU to prioritize different types of SNA traffic

- Router compression
  - Bandwidth solves many problems

Routers have the capability of prioritizing various types of traffic. Filters are typically used to categorize information. We have already discussed DLSw priority implementations. The most popular and easiest method for prioritizing SNA traffic is to install a simple global priority filter. If you need to provide SNA traffic as a high priority, simply filter the TCP port that your router is using for DLSw. The well-known RFC 1434 ports are 2065 and 2067 and are the default DLSw ports used by many implementations. This is a simple way to identify and establish all your SNA connections. RFCs 1795 and 2166 (which supersede the original RFC) provides an option to select a DLSw port for the router. In either case, your challenge will be in determining which port your DLSw traffic will use and put that into a high-priority cue to ensure all SNA traffic goes into that cue.

One of my favorite ways of achieving a greater performance within a network is to turn on the various compression algorithms that are available. Today routers, along with DSUs, offer compression capabilities. Adding more bandwidth solves many performance problems. Being able to take a 56KB line and, through compression, provide at least 128 kilobits to that location may very well save future problems and improve the response time of your end users. This is a very powerful option and one I highly recommend using.

DLSw Performance, Frame Sizes

150

DLSw Performance, Frame Sizes

- Common MTU size between endstations
  - MTU of TR MTU of DLSw versus MTU of SYNC line
    - Reduce segmentation
- MAXDATA versus parameter in SNA limits the SNA frame
  - Normally set for 265 or 521 for SDLC controller
  - 2K for Token Ring devices
  - Does not affect packaging

Some of performance problems that I have encountered with DLSw involve using several packet sizes within the network. Different sizes may cause the routers to segment traffic, adding to network latency. Make sure that a common frame size is used between the two routers to handle the largest frame from either the host or the remote device. Also ensure that the host and remote device use a common packet size. This can be done by properly configuring the MAXDATA parameter on the host.

Coordinating the MTU size or the packet size of these individual devices can greatly improve the performance of the network. I typically recommend a maximum RU size of 521 of an SDLC controller when configuring the MAXDATA parameters. This almost always ensures that segmentation will not happen across the network or between the two endstations. Some older controllers may only support 265, so keep that in mind when you are determining the MAXDATA size.

Appendix: DLSw Configuration Notes

Index

A

acknowledgment timers, 113

activating network resources, 41

Adaptive Rate Based (APR) protocol, 187

address formats, 49–68

  FIDs (Format Identifiers), 51, 52–53, 61

  path identifiers, 57–58

  PU1 traffic support, 53

  Request/Response Header (RH), 54, 62

  Request/Response Unit (RU), 54, 63

  routable address information and, 59

  SNA Network Interconnection (SNI), 66

  Transmission Header (TH), 54, 56, 60

  transmission paths and, 68

Advanced Peer-to-Peer Networking (APPN).
See APPN (Advanced Peer-to-Peer
Networking)

all-routes broadcasts, 104–105

ANR (Automatic Network Routing), 188, 211

AppleTalk, 129

application definitions, 46

APPN (Advanced Peer-to-Peer Networking),
181–193, 200, 203, 211–212

  architecture, 7–8

  Automatic Network Routing (ANR),
188, 211

  Control Point (CP) sessions, 184

  data flow control and, 187

  Dependent LU Requester (DLUR), 191,
192, 211

  Dependent LU Server (DLUS), 191,
192, 211

  High-Performance Routing (HPR), 185,
186, 187, 211, 212

  Intermediate Session Routing (ISR), 185

  network services provided by, 191

  nodes, 183–184

  PU2.1 devices, 37

  Rapid Transport Protocol (RTP), 186,
189, 211

  session establishment, 190

  transmission reliability, 23

ARB (Adaptive Rate Based) protocol, 187

architecture, SNA, 7–8

AS/400, node support by, 37, 53

ATM protocol, 91

Automatic Network Routing (ANR), 188, 211

B

BAN (Boundary Access Node). *See*
Boundary Access Node (BAN)

Banyon Vines, 129

Basic Information Unit (BIU), 64

Basic Transmission Unit (BTU), 64–65

BIND requests, 74–75

BIU (Basic Information Unit), 64

BNN (Boundary Network Node). *See*
Boundary Network Node (BNN)

Boundary Access Node (BAN)
DLSw configuration and, 140–141
frame formats for, 176
SNA frame relay and, 172, 175, 209–210

boundary function processing, 42, 49–50,
53, 61

Boundary Network Node (BNN)
DLSw configuration and, 140–141

Boundary Network Node (BNN), *Continued*
frame formats, 174
SNA frame relay, 172, 173, 209–210

boundary node transmissions, 52–53

bridging, source route. *See* source route
bridging (SRB)

broadcasts, 121–122, 138

BTU (Basic Transmission Unit), 64–65

Bus and Tag connections, 80, 96

C

CANUREACH frame, 138, 143–144, 150

chaining of messages, 62

channel connection definitions, 46

channel gateways, 101–102

channel links, 79, 80–81
parallel channel, 80
series channel, 80

Class of Service (CoS) protocol, 26, 57–58, 67

communications connections, mainframe,
80–81, 101–102

compression, data, 156

configuration, DLSw, 140–141, 223–229

CONTACT command, 146

CONTACTED command, 146

controller positioning, 101–102

controllers, terminal, 44

Control Point (CP) sessions, 184

control sessions, 72

CoS (Class of Service) protocol, 26, 57–58, 67

Cyclic redundancy check (CRC), 19, 21–22

D

data flow. *See also* priority queues
APPN and, 187
CoS (Class of Service) protocol, 26, 57–58,
67
DLSw and, 148
MultiSystem Network Facility (MSNF),
26–27
pacing parameters, 26, 67
SNA Network Interconnection (SNI), 27

Datalink Control protocol, 88

Datalink Switching. *See* DLSw

DecNet, 129

definite responses, 62, 74

Dependent LU Requester (DLUR), 191,
192, 211

Dependent LU Server (DLUS), 191, 192, 211

design considerations, 215
host-centric processing, 216–217
TN3270 and DLSw, 218–219

destination MAC SDLC parameter, 227–228

Direction indicator, 62

distributed processing, history of, 29–30

DLSw, 119, 129–171
bandwith management by, 163–164

broadcasts, elimination of, 138
configuration options, 140–141, 223–231
  frame sizes and, 231
  installation, 223–224
  parameters, 225–228
  performance and priority, 230
  single switch, 140–141, 173
  worksheet for, 229
extended source route bridging and, 139
frames and, 152–153, 231
integration summary, 170–171
investment protection by, 130–131
parameters, 225–226, 227–228
priority implementations, 230
router data compression, 156
scaling and interoperability, 134–135, 161
SDLC control units, 165
sessions
  data transmission, 148
  endstation discovery, 143–144
  local termination, 148
  session initiation, 145
SNA packet overhead and, 154–155
SNA routing and, 136–137
summary and recommendations, 200, 203,
  207–208
TN3270 server and, 218–219
vendor-specific enhancements, 162
versions of, 166, 167, 168–169
WAN access enhancement, 132–133
DLUR (Dependent LU Requester), 191,
  192, 211
DLUS (Dependent LU Server), 191, 192, 211
dumb terminals, 39, 45

E
element addresses, 56, 59
emulators, 214, 218
encapsulation protocol, 157–158
End Node (EN), 183, 184
end-to-end flow control, DLSw, 149
enhanced source route bridging, 123–124
enveloping protocol, 159–160. *See also*
  Boundary Access Node (BAN); Boundary
  Network Node (BNN)
error checking, 19, 21–22, 23
ESCON connections, 80, 96
Ethernet technologies. *See* LAN technologies
exception responses, 62, 74
explicit routes, 9, 57–58

F
FDDI protocol, 91
feeds, 33
FEPs (Front End Processors). *See* Front End
  Processors (FEPs)
FIDs (Format Identifiers)
  FID0, 51
  FID1, 51
  FID2, 49, 52–53, 60, 61, 62, 68
  FID3, 51, 53
  FID4, 49, 51, 52, 56, 57–58, 62, 68, 69
  FID5, 51
  fields and headers, 54–55, 62, 63
  SNA transmission paths and, 68
fields, FID, 54–55
  for FID2, 60, 61
  for FID4, 57–58, 59
  Request/Response Header (RH), 54, 62

fields, FID, *Continued*
  Request/Response Unit (RU), 54, 63
  Transmission Header (TH), 54
Format Identifiers (FIDs). *See* FIDs (Format Identifiers)
FRAD (frame relay access device), 87
Frame Check Sequence (FCS), 21–22
frame formats, 49–52
  Basic Information Unit (BIU), 64
  Basic Transmission Unit (BTU), 64–65
  Boundary Access Node (BAN), 176
  Boundary Network Node (BNN), 174
  DLSw, 152–153, 231
  encapsulation protocols, 157–158
  enveloping protocols, 159–160
  fields or headers in, 54–55
  Path Information Unit (PIU), 64–65
Frame Relay Access Device (FRAD), 87, 141
frame relays, 87, 172–180, 200, 203, 209–210
  BAN-bridged, 175–176
  BNN-routed, 173
  FEP connections and, 178
  LLC2 overhead, 177
  RFC 1490, 172–180
  router connections, 179
Front End Processors (FEPs), 10, 39, 42–43, 46, 66
  boundary function processing, 42, 49–50, 53
  connecting to multiple lines, 82–83
  frame relays and, 178
  LAN Gateway 3745 and, 96–97
  links between, 82–83, 84
  remote line concentration and, 17
  routing and, 9, 42–43

full-duplex sessions, 86
Function Management Header (FMH), 63

G

gateways, 194–200, 203, 213–214
  channel, 101–102
  FIDs and, 52–53
  LAN Gateway 3172, 98
  LAN Gateway 3174, 98
  LAN Gateway 3745, 96–97
  OSA-2 adapter, 81, 98–99
  positioning of, 101–102
  SAA IPX, 195, 199, 200, 203, 213
  terminal controllers and, 44
  TN3270(E), 119, 196–197, 198, 199, 200, 203, 213
  Web browsers and, 119, 198, 199, 203, 213–214, 218–219
global parameters, DLSw, 225–226

H

half-duplex sessions, 75, 86
headers, FID, 54–55
  Request/Response Header (RH), 54, 62
  Request/Response Unit (RU), 54, 63
  Transmission Header (TH), 54
high network priority queues, 67
High-Performance Routing (HPR), 185, 186, 187, 211, 212
host-centric processing, 28, 216–217

I

ICANREACH frame, 138, 144, 150
IDBLK SDLC parameter, 228
IDNUM SDLC parameter, 228
inactivating network resources, 41

installation, DLSw, 223–224

integration technologies, 119–200, 203, 215, 216–217

   APPN (Advanced Peer-to-Peer Networking), 119, 181–193, 200, 203, 211–212

   DLSw, 119, 129–171, 207–208, 223–231

   frame relays, 79, 87, 172–180, 200, 203, 209–210

   gateways, 119, 194–200, 203, 213–214

   IP encapsulation, 119, 127–128, 200, 203

   SDLC encapsulation, 119, 125–126, 200, 203

   source route bridging (SRB), 119, 120–124, 200, 203

Intermediate Session Routing (ISR), 185

Internetwork, 5–6

IP encapsulation, 119, 200, 203

IPX SAA gateways, 195, 200, 203, 213

IPX/SPX protocol, 23

ISR (Intermediate Session Routing), 185

K

keep-alive timers, 89, 111–112

L

LAN Gateway 3172, 98

LAN Gateway 3174, 98

LAN Gateway 3745, 96–97

LAN technologies, 18

   ATM protocol, 91

   Datalink Control protocol, 88

   DLSw integration and, 130–133

   Ethernet protocol, 91

   FDDI protocol, 91

   gateways, 96–97, 98–99

   interfaces, 100

   LLC1 protocol, 88, 107

   LLC2 protocol, 21–22, 88–89, 107, 108–113

   session establishment, 150–151

   Token Ring protocol, 21, 79, 90, 103, 104–105

leads, 33

legacy technologies, 204–206

   IP encapsulation, 119, 200, 203

   SDLC encapsulation, 119, 125–126, 200, 203

   source route bridging (SRB), 119, 120–124, 142, 203

LEN device, 184

library, node definition, 46

limitations, SNA network, 116

line resources, 46

links, 79–91

   ATM protocol, 91

   channel, 79, 80–81

   Datalink Control protocol, 88

   Ethernet protocol, 91

   FDDI protocol, 91

   FEPs (Front End Processors) and, 82–83

   frame relay protocol, 79, 87

   LLC1 protocol, 88, 107

   LLC2 protocol, 21–22, 88–89, 107, 108–113

   SDLC protocol, 79, 84–86, 114, 130–131, 150–151, 165

   Token Ring protocol, 21, 79, 90, 103, 104–105

   X.25 protocol, 87

LLC1 protocol, 88, 107

LLC2 protocol, 21–22, 88–89, 107, 108–113
connection activation, 115
datalink switching and, 142
DLSw integration and, 130–133
Ethernet session initiation, 150
SNA activation and connection, 115
SNA frame relay overhead, 177
timers, 89, 109–110, 111–112, 113
LLC (Logical Link Control), 107
LOCADDR parameter, 61
local addresses, 61
Local Session Format Identifier
(LSFID), 185
Logical Link Control 1 (LLC1). See LLC1
protocol
Logical Link Control 2 (LLC2). See LLC2
protocol
Logical Link Control (LLC), 107
Logical Unit (LU) sessions, 73, 74–75
Logical Units (LUs), 37–38, 39, 41, 72
LOGOFF requests, 41
LOGON requests, 41
Low Entry Networking (LEN) device, 184
LSFID (Local Session Format Identifier), 185
LU resources, 46
LUs (logical units), 37–38, 39, 41, 72
LU-to-LU sessions, 73, 74–75

M

mainframes
APPN SNA architecture, 7–8
communications connections, 80–81
and growth on SNA networks, 6
Legacy SNA architecture, 7
sessions and transactions, 24–25

VTAM software, 39
Major Node Definitions, 46
MAXDATA parameter, 227
memory requirements, 161, 188
microcode, 44
modems, 11–12
MSNF protocol, 26–27
Multicast support, 169
multidrop technology, 15–16, 85–86
multiline transmission groups, 82–83
multipoint technology, 15–16
multiport bridges, 123
MultiSystem Network Facility (MSNF),
26–27

N

NAUs (Network Addressable Units). See
Network Addressable Units (NAUs)
NCP (Network Control Program). See Front
End Processors (FEPs)
Network Addressable Units (NAUs), 49–68
FIDs (Format Identifiers), 51, 52–53, 61
path identifiers, 57–58
PU1 traffic support, 53
Request/Response Header (RH), 54, 62
Request/Response Unit (RU), 54, 63
routable address information and, 59
SNA Network Interconnection (SNI), 66
SNA transmission paths and, 68
Transmission Header (TH), 54, 56, 60
network-centric processing, 31–32
Network Control Program (NCP), 42–43, 66
network management, APPN services, 191
Network Node (NN), 183, 184
network resource activation, 41

NIC (network interface card), 101–102
nodes, 37–38, 39
    activating/inactivating with SSCP, 41
    Boundary Access Node (BAN)
        DLSw configuration and, 140–141
        frame formats, 176
        SNA frame relay, 172, 175, 209–210
    Boundary Network Node (BNN)
        DLSw configuration and, 140–141
        frame formats for, 174
        SNA frame relay and, 172, 173, 209–210
    End (EN), 183, 184
    LENs, 184
    links between, 79–91
    Network (NN), 183, 184
    PU1, 37, 53
    PU2, 37, 39, 44
    PU2.1, 37
    PU4, 37, 39, 42
    PU5, 37, 39, 40
    session establishment and, 190
    in SNA hierarchy, 39
    support of LUs by, 37–38
nonroutable frames, 49–50
nonroutable protocol, SNA as, 9
no response notifications, 19, 62
normal network priority queues, 67
NRZ/NRZI SDLC parameter, 227

O

OSA-2 adapter, 81, 98–99
overhead
    DLSw and, 208
    encapsulation and, 158
    enveloping and, 159–160

P

pacing parameters, 26, 67
parallel channels, 80
parameters, DLSw, 225–228
path identifiers, 57–58
Path Information Unit (PIU), 64–65
peer address, DLSw, 225–226
performance considerations, DLSw, 230, 231
PIU (Path Information Unit), 64–65
poll addresses, 15–16, 227
poll frames, 109–110, 111–112, 113
priority queues, 57–58
    Class of Service (CoS) protocol, 26,
        57–58, 67
    DLSw prioritization, 136–137, 163–164
    high network priority, 67
    low network priority, 67
    normal network priority, 67
processing environments
    distributed, 29–30
    host-centric, 28
    network-centric, 31–32
processor speeds, 161, 188, 207–208
PU1 node, 37, 53
PU2.1 nodes, 37
PU2 node, 37, 39, 44
PU4 node, 37, 39, 42
PU5 node, 37, 39, 40
PUs (Physical Units), 37–38, 39, 41, 46, 72.
    See also specific PUs
PUT5 node, 37, 39, 40

R

Rapid Transport Protocol (RTP), 186,
    189, 211

REACH_ACK frame, 144

Receiver Readies (RRs), 146

   T1 timers and, 109–110

   T2 timers and, 113

   Ti timers and, 111–112

remote line concentration, 17

Request for Comments (RFC) standards,
   134–135

Request/Response Header (RH), 54, 62

Request/Response Unit (RU), 54, 63

rerouting, benefits of DLSw and, 136

resources

   activation of network, 41

   Major Node Definitions, 46

   NAUs (Network Addressable Units), 49–50

responses modes, 62, 74

RFC 1434, 166

RFC 1490, 172–180, 209–210

RFC 1795, 167

RFC 2166, 168–169

RH (Request/Response Header), 54, 62

RIF (Routing Information Field), 106

routable frames, 49–50, 59

routers. *See also* DLSw

   ANR (Automatic Network Routing), 188

   DLSw and data compression, 156

   FEPs as, 42–43

   frame relay connections and, 179

   priority queues and, 163–164

Routing Information Field (RIF), 106

routing, subarea, 9, 59, 66, 96–97, 136

RR poll frames

   T1 timers and, 109–110

   T2 timers and, 113

   Ti timers and, 111–112

RTP/ANR protocol, 23, 186, 189

RU (Request/Response Unit), 54, 63

S

SAA IPX gateways, 195, 200, 203, 213

SABME command, 88, 106, 115, 146

SAP tables, DLSw, 225–226

scaling, DLSw and, 134–135, 161

SDLC encapsulation, 119, 125–126,
   200, 203

SDLC multidrop, 15–16, 85–86

SDLC parameters, 227–228

SDLC protocol, 15–16, 19, 79

   DLSw integration and, 130–131, 165

   SDLC multidrop, 15–16, 85–86

   session establishment, 150–151

   switched line activation, 114

   WAN networks and, 84

Send/Receive protocols, 75, 106

series channels, 80

Service Access Point (SAP), 173

sessions, 24–25, 71–75, 143–151

   APPN establishment of, 190

   BIND requests and, 74–75

   control, 72

   DLSw

      data transmission, 148

      endstation discovery, 143–144

      local termination, 148

      session initiation, 145

   Ethernet initiation, 150–151

   half-duplex, 75

   LU-to-LU, 73

   SDLC initiation of, 150–151

   SSCP-to-LU, 72

SSCP-to-PU, 72

Token Ring protocol
discovery/initiation by, 104–105, 143–149
setup by, 106
VTAM software and, 41

Set Asynchronous Balanced Mode Extended
(SABME), 88, 106, 115

Set Normal Response Mode Extended
(SNRME), 84

Set Normal Response Mode (SNRM), 84,
114, 150

Shielded Twisted Pair technology (STP), 103

single-route broadcasts, 104–105

single switch DLSw configuration, 140–141,
173

SNA Architecture Guide, 55

SNA frame relays. *See* frame relays

SNA gateways. *See* gateways

SNA links. *See* links

SNA Network Interconnection (SNI), 27, 66

SNA nodes. *See* nodes

SNA sessions. *See* sessions

SNI protocol, 27

SNRME (Set Normal Response Mode
Extended), 84

SNRM (Set Normal Response Mode), 84,
114, 150

source MAC SDLC parameter, 227–228

source route bridging (SRB), 119, 120–124,
200, 203
broadcasts and, 121–122
datalink switching and, 142
DLSw extension of, 139
enhanced, 123–124

Spanning Tree protocol, 104

SRB (source route bridging). *See* source route
bridging (SRB)

SRT (Symbol Resolution Table), 59

SSCP (System Services Control Point), 41

SSCP-to-LU sessions, 46, 72

SSCP-to-PU sessions, 46, 72

SSP (Switch-to-Switch protocol), 142

subareas, 40
FID4 identifier and, 52, 57, 59
nodes and, 51, 57, 59
routing from, 9, 59, 66, 96–97

switched node definitions, 46

Switch-to-Switch protocol (SSP), 142,
152–153

Symbol Resolution Table (SRT), 59

SYSGEN process, 43

T

T1 connections, 82–83

T1 timers, 89, 109–110

T2 timers, 113

TCP/IP protocol, 5–6
datalink switching and, 142
DLSw frame format, 152–153
reliability of transmissions, 23
SNA packet overhead, 154–155

terminal controllers, 44

terminals, SNA hierarchy and, 39, 45

termination, session, 148

TEST frames, 143–144

3270 controller, 45. *See also* PU2 node

3270 device, 39, 45

TH (Transmission Header), 54, 56, 60

timers
DLSw RFC 2166 and, 168–169

timers, *Continued*
    T1, 89, 109–110
    T2, 113
    Ti, 89, 111–112
Ti timers, 89, 111–112
TN3270, 213, 218–219
TN3270(E), 119, 196–197, 198, 199, 200,
    203, 213
Token Ring protocol, 7, 21, 79, 90, 103
    DLSw integration and, 130–133
    session discovery/initiation, 104–105,
        143–149
    session setup, 106
traditional channel links, 79
transactions, 24–25
Transmission Groups, 82
Transmission Header (TH), 54, 56, 60

U

unnumbered acknowledgment (UA), 146
Unshielded Twisted Pair technology
    (UTP), 103

V

virtual path identifiers, 57–58
virtual routes, 9, 57–58

VTAMLST library, 46
VTAM software
    FID format, 52–53
    sign-on screen, 72
    in SNA hierarchy, 39, 40
    SSCP functions and, 41

W

WAN technologies, 7, 18, 84
    DLSw integration and, 132–133
    frame relay protocol. *See* frame relays
    link protocols, 84
    SDLC protocol, 15–16, 19, 79
    X.25 protocol, 19, 87
Web browser gateways, 119, 198, 199, 203,
    213–214, 218–219
Wide Area Network (WAN). *See* WAN
    technologies

X

X.25 protocol, 19, 87
XID frames, 104, 106, 114, 145, 150

CUSTOMER NOTE: IF THIS BOOK IS ACCOMPANIED BY SOFTWARE, PLEASE READ THE FOLLOWING BEFORE OPENING THE PACKAGE.

To use this DISK, your system must meet the following requirements:

Platform/Processor/Operating System. Windows 3.1 or higher

RAM. 16MB

Hard Drive Space. 2MB

Peripherals. PowerPoint 97 (or viewer)